MATHEMATICS
OF THE SECURITIES
INDUSTRY

William A. Rini

McGraw-Hill
New York   Chicago   San Francisco   Lisbon
London   Madrid   Mexico City   Milan   New Delhi
San Juan   Seoul   Singapore   Sydney   Toronto

The McGraw-Hill Companies

1 2 3 4 5 6 7 8 9 0   DOC/DOC   0 9 8 7 6 5 4 3

ISBN 0-07-141316-2

Printed and bound by R.R. Donnelley.

McGraw-Hill books are available at special quantity
discounts to use as premiums and sales promotions, or for
use in corporate training programs. For more information,
please write to the Director of Special Sales, Professional
Publishing, McGraw-Hill, Two Penn Plaza, New York, NY
10121-2298. Or contact your local bookstore.

 This book is printed on recycled, acid-free paper
containing a minimum of 50% recycled, de-inked fiber.

To Catherine . . .

my GOOD wife

my BETTER half

my BEST friend

HOW THIS BOOK
CAN HELP YOU

Solve Two of the Toughest Problems When Preparing for the Stockbroker's Exam

Those wishing to become licensed as stockbrokers must pass the series 7 examination. This exam, known officially as the General Securities Registered Representative Examination, is very rigorous. Traditionally, students without a financial background have a difficult time with the mathematical calculations peculiar to the world of stocks, bonds, and options. Many are also relatively unfamiliar with proper use of the calculator and thus are doubly hampered in their efforts to become registered.

This book will help you to overcome both problems. It not only simplifies the math; it also shows you how to make an effective tool of the calculator.

Increase Control Over Your Own (or Your Clients') Investments

Investors (and licensed stockbrokers) have the same problems. For example, they need to know

- *How much buying power there is in a margin account*
- *What a portfolio is worth*
- *How to calculate a P/E ratio*
- *The amount of accrued interest on a debt security*
- *How to compare a tax-free and a taxable yield*
- *Whether a dividend is due to a stockholder*
- *How to read—and understand—a balance sheet*

These and many other questions—all critical to successful investing—can be answered only by employing the proper calculations. While such skills are absolutely necessary for the stockbroker, they are also of inestimable value to the individual investor.

Mathematics of the Securities Industry is the book to refer to both before and after taking the series 7 exam. It covers all the mathematics you need to master to pass the exams for brokerage licensing and other NASD/NYSE licensing, including the series 6 (mutual funds/variable annuities), series 52 (municipal securities), and the series 62 (corporate securities), among others.

After the examination, it serves as an excellent quick reference for most important financial calculations necessary to monitoring stock and bond investments.

How to Use This Book

Each type of calculation is presented in a clear and consistent format:

1. The explanation briefly describes the purpose of the calculation, the reason for it, and how it is best used.
2. The general formula is then presented.
3. The example (and sometimes a group of several examples) shows you how to do the computation and enables you to verify that you are calculating it correctly.
4. The calculator guide provides step-by-step, detailed instructions for using a simple calculator to solve the formula.
5. How do you know you understand the computation? A self-test (with the answers provided) enables you to assure yourself that you can perform the calculation correctly.

You may take advantage of this format in a number of ways. Those of you with little or no financial background should go through each step. Those of you who are comfortable with the calculator may skip step 4. The advanced student may only go through step 1 (or steps 1 and 2) and step 5.

Note: All calculations may be done by hand, with pencil and paper. Using a simple calculator, while not absolutely necessary, makes things simpler, more accurate, and much quicker. Only a simple calculator is required—nothing elaborate or costly.

A valuable extra is that many of the chapters have an added "Practical Exercise" section. The questions in these exercises are posed so as to simulate actual market situations. You are thus able to test your knowledge under "battle conditions." In many instances the answers to these exercises—in the "Answers to Practical Exercises" section of the text (just after Chapter 26)—contain very practical and useful information not covered in the chapters themselves.

How to Use the Calculator

I used a Texas Instruments hand-held calculator, Model TI-1795+, for this book. It is solar-powered, requiring no batteries, only a light source. This calculator has

- *A three-key memory function* (M+, M−, Mrc)
- *A reverse-sign key* (+/−)
- *A combination on/clear-entry/clear key* (on/c)

While the memory function and the reverse-sign key are helpful, they are not absolutely necessary. Any simple calculator may be used.

Turning on the Calculator

When the calculator is off, the answer window is completely blank. (The TI-1795+ has an automatic shutoff feature; that is, it turns itself off approximately 10 minutes after it has been last used.) To turn on the calculator, simply press the on/c button (for "on/clear"). The calculator display should now show 0. [On some calculators there are separate on/off keys, c (for "clear"), and c/e (for "clear entry") keys.]

"Erasing" a Mistake

You do not have to completely clear the calculator if you make a mistake. You can clear just the last digits entered with either the ce (clear entry) button if your calculator has one or the on/c (on/clear) button if your calculator is so equipped. If you make an error while doing a calculation, you can "erase" just the last number entered rather than starting all over again.

Example: You are attempting to add four different numbers 2369 - 4367 - 1853 and 8639. You enter 2369, then the + key, then 4367, then the + key, then 1853, then the + key, and then you enter the last number as

8693 rather than 8639. If you realize your error before
you hit the equals sign, you can change the last number you entered by hitting the on/c (or c/e) key and
then reentering the correct number.

Let's practice correcting an error. Enter 2, then +,
then 3. There's the error—you entered 3 instead of 4! The
calculator window now reads 3. To correct the last digit—
to change the 3 to a 4—press one of the following buttons
once:

- *on/c*
- *c*
- *c/ce*

Remember, press this button only *once*. Notice that the
calculator window now reads 2. Pressing the on/c button
"erased" only the last number you entered, the number 3,
but left everything else. The 2 and the + are still entered
in the calculator! Now press 4 and then =. The window
now reads, correctly, 6.

For such a simple calculation this seems really not
worth the bother. But imagine how frustrated you would
be if you were adding a very long list of figures and then
made an error. Without the "clear" key, you would need
to start all over again. So long as you have not hit the =
key after you input the incorrect number, you can simply
erase the last digits entered (the wrong numbers) and
replace them with the correct number.

Clearing the Calculator

Clearing a calculator is similar to erasing a blackboard: All
previous entries are erased, or "cleared." Each new calculation should be performed on a "cleared" calculator, just
as you should, for example, write on a clean blackboard.

You know the calculator is cleared when the answer
window shows 0. Most calculators are cleared after they
are turned on. If *anything* other than 0. shows, the calculator is not cleared. You must press one of the following
buttons twice, depending on how your calculator is
equipped:

- *on/c*
- *c*
- *c/ce*

This erases everything you have entered into the calculator. When you begin the next computation, it will be with a "clean slate."

Example: Let's return to the preceding example. Enter 2, then +, then 3. The window shows 3, the last number entered. Now press the on/c key. The window now shows "2." At this point you have erased just the last number entered, the 2 and the + are still there. Now press the on/c button a second time. The window now reads 0. The calculator is now completely cleared.

Clearing Memory

Calculators with a memory function have several buttons, usually labeled "M+," "M−," and "Mr/c." When the memory function is in use, the letter M appears in the calculator window, usually in the upper left corner. To clear the memory, press the Mr/c button *twice*. This should eliminate the M from the display. If any numbers remain, they can be cleared by pressing the on/c button, once or twice, until the calculator reads 0.

Just as some baseball players have a ritual they perform before their turn at bat, many calculator users have a ritual before doing a calculation—they hit the Mr/c button twice, then the on/c (or c or c/ce) twice. This is a good habit to acquire—it ensures that the calculator is truly cleared.

The proper use of the memory function is detailed several times throughout the text.

Calculator Guides

Almost all the formulas described in this book include very specific calculator instructions, "Calculator Guides." You should be able to skip these instructions after you have done a number of calculations successfully, but they will be there should you need them.

These "Calculator Guides" are complete; they show you exactly which buttons to press, and in what sequence, to arrive at the correct answer. Each "Calculator Guide" section starts with an arrowhead (▶), which indicates that you should clear your calculator. When you see this symbol, be sure that the calculator window shows only 0. No other digits, nor the letter M, should appear.

Following the arrowhead are the buttons to press. Press only the buttons indicated. The second arrowhead (◀) indicates that the calculation is completed and that the numbers following it, always in bold, show the correct answer. The figures in bold will be exactly the numbers that will appear in your calculator's window!

After the bold numbers there will be numbers in parentheses that will "translate" the answer into either dollars and cents or percent, and/or round the answer appropriately.

Example: Multiply $2.564 and $85.953.

> ▶ 2.564 × 85.953 = ◀ **220.38349** ($220.38)

Try it! Follow the instructions in the line above on your calculator.

- *Clear the calculator.*
- *Enter the numbers, decimal points, and arithmetic signs exactly as indicated:* 2.564 × 85.953 =.
- *Your calculator display should read* **220.38349**—this translates and rounds to $220.38

Let's try something a little more complicated.

Example: $\dfrac{45.98}{346} \times \dfrac{197.45}{93.4}$

The problem may be solved longhand by first multiplying the two top numbers and then dividing the resulting figure first by one bottom number and then by the other bottom number. There are a few other methods as well, but let's see how fast and simple it is by using the calculator. Here are the instructions:

CALCULATOR GUIDE

▶ 45.98 × 197.45 ÷ 346 ÷ 93.4 = ◀ **0.2809332** (0.28)

If you didn't arrive at that answer, redo the calculation precisely according to the "Calculator Guide" instructions. Note that you only need hit the = key once. If you enter the numbers and signs *exactly* as called for in the calculator guide, you will arrive at the correct answer!

SELF-TEST

Perform the following calculations. Write your answers down, and then check them against the correct answers given at the end of this section. And don't go pressing any extra = keys! Only hit the = key when and if the calculator guide says so.

A. ▶ .945 ÷ 56.96 = ◀
B. ▶ 854 × 65.99 = ◀
C. ▶ 56.754 × 92.532 ÷ 5229 = ◀
D. ▶ 23 − 6.5 × 88 = ◀
E. ▶ 54.9 + 23.458 × 95 ÷ 64.11 = ◀

ANSWERS TO SELF-TEST

A. 0.0165905
B. 56355.46
C. 1.0043146
D. 1452.
E. 116.11308

If you did the problems correctly, even though not until the second or third try, you will have no trouble doing any of the calculations in this book.

Rounding Off

Most Wall Street calculations require that you show only two digits to the right of the decimal place, for example, 98.74 rather than 98.74285.

To round off to two decimal places, you must examine the third digit to the right of the decimal.

- *If the third digit to the right of the decimal is less than 5 (4, 3, 2, 1, or 0), then ignore all digits after the second one to the right of the decimal.*

  Example: In the number 98.74285, the third digit after the decimal point is 2 (less than 5). You reduce the number to 98.74

- *If the third digit after the decimal is 5 or more (5, 6, 7, 8, or 9), increase the second digit after the decimal by one.*

Example: In the number 67.12863, the third digit after the decimal is 8 (5 or more). So you increase the second postdecimal digit by one, changing the second digit, 2, to a 3! The rounded number becomes 67.13.

Not all computations require two digits after the decimal. Whatever the requirement, the rounding-off process is basically the same. For instance, to round off to a whole number, examine the first digit after the decimal.

- *If it is 4 or less, ignore all the digits after the decimal point.*

Example: To round 287.382 to a whole number, examine the first digit after the decimal (3). Since it is 4 or less, reduce the number to 287.

- *If the first digit after the decimal is 5 or greater, increase the number immediately before the decimal by 1.*

Example: Round off 928.519. Because the first digit after the decimal is 5 (more than 4), you add 1 to the number just before the decimal place: 928.519 is rounded off to 929.

Some numbers seem to jump greatly in value when rounded upward.

Example: Round 39.6281 to a whole number. It becomes 40! Round 2699.51179 to a whole number. It becomes 2700!

SELF-TEST

Round the following numbers to two decimal places.

A. 1.18283
B. 1.1858
C. 27.333
D. 27.3392
E. 817.391
F. 7289.99499

ANSWERS TO SELF-TEST

A. 1.18
B. 1.19
C. 27.33
D. 27.34

E. 817.39

F. 7289.99

Chain Calculations

A useful timesaver when using the calculator is chain multiplication and division. It comes into play when you have to

- *Multiply a given number by several other numbers*
- *Divide several numbers by the same number*

Example: You have a series of multiplication problems with a single multiplier.

$$31.264 \times .095 \quad 31.264 \times 2.73 \quad 31.264 \times 95.1$$

To solve all these calculations, you can enter the figure 31.264 only once. It is not necessary to clear the calculator between problems.

CALCULATOR GUIDE

▶ $31.264 \times .095 =$ ◀ **2.97008**

Then, after noting this answer, *and without clearing the calculator,* enter

$2.73 =$ ◀ **85.35072**

Then, after noting *this* answer, and again without clearing the calculator, enter

$95.1 =$ ◀ **2973.2064**

and *that's* the answer to the final multiplication.

If you had to repeat the common multiplicand for all three operations, you would have had to press 36 keys. The "chain" feature reduces that number to just 22—a real timesaver that also decreases the chances of error.

Let's see how chain *division* works. You have three different calculations to do, each with the same divisor.

$$31.58 \div 3.915 \quad 4769.773 \div 3.915 \quad .63221 \div 3.915$$

You can solve all three problems by entering the figure 3.915 and the division sign ($\div$) only once.

▶ $31.58 \div 3.915 =$ ◀ **8.0664112**

Then, after noting the answer, *and without clearing the calculator*, enter

$$4769.773 = \blacktriangleleft 1218.3328$$

Then, after noting *this* answer, and again without clearing the calculator, enter

$$.63221 = \blacktriangleleft 0.161484$$

and *that's* the answer to the final division. Saves a lot of time, doesn't it?

CONTENTS

PRICING STOCKS

Dollars and Fractions versus Dollars and Cents

Stocks traditionally were priced (quoted) in dollars and sixteenths of dollars, but that changed in the fairly recent past. The United States was the world's last major securities marketplace to convert to the decimal pricing system (cents rather than fractions). The changeover was done in increments between mid-2000 and mid-2001. Interestingly, many *bonds* are still quoted in fractions rather than decimals.

> *Example:* In today's market, a stock worth $24.25 a share is quoted as "24.25." Note that stock prices are not preceded by a dollar sign ($); it is simply understood that the price is in dollars and cents. Under the older fraction system, this price, 24.25, used to be shown as "24$^{1}/_{4}$."

Stock price changes are now measured in pennies rather than fractions. Prior to the year 2000, a stock closing at a price of 38 on a given day and then closing at 38$^{1}/_{2}$ on the following day was said to have gone "up $^{1}/_{2}$." Today we say that the first day's closing price would be shown as 38.00, the second day's closing price would be 38.50, and the net change would be "up .50."

Most security exchanges permit price changes as small as 1 cent, so there may be four different prices between 24.00 and 24.05 (24.01, 24.02, 24.03, and 24.04). Some exchanges may limit price changes to 5-cent increments or 10-cent increments. This is particularly true of the options exchanges.

Fractional Pricing

For the record, the old pricing system (fractions) worked in the following fashion. Securities were traded in "eighths" for many generations and then began trading in "sixteenths" in the 1990s. When using eighths, the smallest price variation was $^1/_8$, or $0.125 (12$^1/_2$ cents) per share. When trading began in sixteenths, the smallest variation, $^1/_{16}$, was $0.0625 (6$^1/_4$ cents) per share. Under the decimal system, the smallest variation has shrunk to $0.01 (1 cent) per share. You will need information on fractional pricing when looking up historical price data (prior to 2000), which always were expressed in fractions. Many stocks purchased under the old system of fractions will be sold under the new decimal system, and the old prices must be converted to the decimal system when figuring profits and losses. As a professional, you should be able to work with this fractional system as well.

Fraction	Dollar Equivalent
$^1/_{16}$	$0.0625
$^1/_8$	$0.125
$^3/_{16}$	$0.1875
$^1/_4$	$0.25
$^5/_{16}$	$0.3125
$^3/_8$	$0.375
$^7/_{16}$	$0.4375
$^1/_2$	$0.50
$^9/_{16}$	$0.5625
$^5/_8$	$0.625
$^{11}/_{16}$	$0.6875
$^3/_4$	$0.75
$^{13}/_{16}$	$0.8125
$^7/_8$	$0.875
$^{15}/_{16}$	$0.9375

Note that each fraction is $^1/_{16}$ higher than the previous fraction—higher by 6$^1/_4$ cents!

The vast majority of the people working within the financial community have these fractions memorized. Many of them (particularly government bond traders) know all the fractions in 64ths!

Some of these fractions require no computation. Everyone knows that $^1/_4$ is 25 cents, $^1/_2$ is 50 cents, and $^3/_4$ is 75 cents. The "tougher" ones ($^1/_8$, $^3/_{16}$, $^7/_8$ and $^{15}/_{16}$, for example) are not so tough; they require only a simple calculation. The formula for converting these fractions to dollars and cents is simple: Divide the numerator (the top number of the fraction) by the denominator (the bottom number of the fraction, 8 or 16). The answers will show anywhere from one to four decimal places (numbers to the right of the decimal point).

CALCULATOR GUIDE

Example: To find the dollar equivalent of $1/8$, divide the numerator (1) by the denominator (8):

▶ $1 \div 8 =$ ◀ **0.125** ($12^{1}/_{2}$ cents)

To find the dollar equivalent of $3/16$:

▶ $3 \div 16 =$ ◀ **0.1875** ($18^{3}/_{4}$ cents)

To find the dollar equivalent of $7/8$:

▶ $7 \div 8 =$ ◀ **0.875** ($87^{1}/_{2}$ cents)

To find the dollar equivalent of $15/16$:

▶ $15 \div 16 =$ ◀ **0.9375** ($93^{3}/_{4}$ cents)

Let's convert a few stock prices—expressed in fractions —into dollars and cents. The dollar amounts show the worth of just a single share of stock. Note that in the following conversions, full dollar amounts (no pennies) are carried over as is—you just add two zeroes after the decimal. You arrive at the cents amounts, if any, either by adding the memorized values to the dollar amounts or by means of the preceding calculation. (*Memorizing* them is easier; remember how your school math got a lot easier once you learned your multiplication tables?)

Stock Price Listing	*Dollars and Cents*
24	$24.00
$36^{1}/_{2}$	$36.50
$8^{1}/_{16}$	$8.0625
$109^{7}/_{8}$	$109.875
$55^{9}/_{16}$	$55.5625
$4^{5}/_{8}$	$4.625
$21^{11}/_{16}$	$21.6875
$73^{3}/_{8}$	$73.375

Round Lots, Odd Lots

Each dollar amount in the preceding table shows the value of a single share at the listed price. While it is possible to purchase just one share of stock, most people buy stocks in lots of 100 shares or in a multiple of 100 shares, such as 300, 800, 2,300, or 8,600. These multiples are called *round lots*. Amounts of stock from 1 to 99 shares are called *odd lots*. A 200-share block of stock is a round lot; 58 shares is an odd lot. An example of a *mixed lot* would be 429 shares (a 400-share round lot and an odd lot of 29 shares).

Decimal Pricing

Decimal pricing is a lot simpler. There are no fractions to memorize or calculate, just good old dollars and cents that we are very used to dealing with. See why they switched from fractions? Decimal pricing makes everything easier on traders, investors, and operations personnel—with a much lower opportunity for errors—and puts our markets on a more nearly level playing field with the world's other financial markets, which have been "decimalized" for many years.

To value a given stock holding, simply multiply the number of shares held by the per-share price:

Dollar value = number of shares × per-share price

Example: XYZ stock is selling at 36.55 per share. One hundred shares of XYZ would be worth $3,655:

100 shares × 36.55 = 3,655

Two hundred shares of ABC at 129.88 per share would be worth $25,976:

200 shares × 129.88 = 25,976

Example: What is the current value of 250 shares of CDE stock selling at 37.27 per share?

250 × 37.27 = $9,317.50

CALCULATOR GUIDE

▶ 250 × 37.27 = ◀ **9317.5** ($9,317.50)

Note: The calculator did not show the final zero; you have to add it.

SELF-TEST

What is the dollar value for the following stock positions?

A. 100 shares @ 23.29
B. 250 shares @ 5.39
C. 2,500 shares @ 34.60
D. 35 shares @ 109
E. What is the *total* dollar value for *all* these positions?

ANSWERS TO SELF-TEST

A. $2,329.00 (100 × 23.29)
B. $1,347.50 (250 × 5.39)
C. $86,500.00 (2,500 × 34.60)
D. $3,815.00 (35 × 109)
E. $93,991.50 (2,329.00 + 1,347.50 + 86,500.00 + 3,815.00)

Chapter 2

PRICING CORPORATE BONDS

While stocks, both common and preferred, are *equity* securities and represent ownership in a corporation, bonds are *debt* securities. A bondholder has, in effect, a debtor/creditor relationship with the corporation or governmental agency that issued the bond. Many stocks pay *dividends;* most bonds pay *interest.* Bonds are quite important in the financial scheme of things. Most of the money raised in the primary market (the new-issue market) is in the form of bonds rather than stocks. Bonds issued by a given company are *safer* than any equity security issued by that same company because their interest must be paid in full before any dividends may be paid on either preferred or common stock. Broadly speaking, bonds are higher on the safety scale than stocks but generally not as rewarding —an example of the risk-reward relationship.

Bond Quotations

Bonds issued by corporations (as opposed to bonds issued by municipalities and the federal government) trade in points and eighths as a percentage of par. One bond is considered to have a par value of $1,000. This means that if you own one bond, the company that issued the bond owes you $1,000 and will pay you that $1,000 when the bond matures. This $1,000 is the bond's *par value,* also called its *face value.* Either term means the amount of the loan represented by the bond, that is, the amount the issuing company has borrowed and must repay when the due date (maturity date) arrives.

It is extremely unlikely that an investor will own just one bond. In fact, it is very rare that bonds are even issued in "pieces" as small as a single bond with a total par value of only $1,000. A corporate bond "round lot" is considered to be 10 bonds, and it is very difficult to find even 5-bond lots. The notation for one bond is "1 M." This means 1 bond of $1,000 par—a total par value of $1,000. Traders and investors call this "one bond," and they would write an order for this bond as "1 M."

When trading bonds, financial people use the letter M to mean one *thousand*, not one million! (Comes from the French and Italian words for "thousand.") A bond with a total par value of $10,000 is written as "10 M," and the lot would be referred to as "10 bonds." A bond with a total par value of $100,000 would be called "100 bonds," written out as "100 M." A quarter-million dollars worth of bonds would be called "250 bonds" and would be written as "250 M."

Even though single bonds (1 M) aren't common, for simplicity's sake, we will use one bond with a total par value of $1,000 in many of our examples. If you are dealing with a 25-bond block, it is a simple matter to treat it as one bond and then to multiply your result by 25 at the end of the calculation.

Bond prices look very different from stock prices, and there are big differences: Stock prices are in dollars and cents, whereas bond prices are expressed as a percentage of par value in fractions.

Example: When a bond is quoted at 98, it is selling not for $98, but for 98 percent of its par value. Since each bond has a par value of $1,000, one bond trading at 98 is worth 98 percent of its $1,000 par value.

$$.98 \ (98\%) \times \$1,000 = \$980$$

If a *stock* is trading at 98, it is worth $98 per share. A corporate *bond* trading at 98 is worth $980!

There are several mathematical methods for converting bond quotes to dollar values. Each of the following methods may be used to convert one bond's (1 M) quoted price into dollars and cents. Use whichever of the following methods works best for you. Each method is demonstrated by example. Before reviewing the examples, you might refer to the fractions shown in the first table in Chapter 1. Just the eighths will do ($1/8$, $3/8$, $5/8$, $7/8$), since most corporate and municipal bonds trade in eighths, not sixteenths.

Example: Find the dollar value of one bond (1 M) quoted at $96^{1}/_{2}$.

Either convert the fraction in the price to a decimal and then move the decimal point one place to the right:

$$96^1/_2 = 96.5$$

Then, moving the decimal one place to the right, 96.5 becomes 965. ($965.00). Or convert the fraction in the price to a decimal, and then multiply by 10:

$$96^1/_2 = 96.5$$

Then multiply by 10 and add a dollar sign:

$$96.5 \times 10 = 965. (\$965.00)$$

I find it best to use the first method. You simply treat the bond price as an old (predecimal) stock price and convert the fraction to a decimal ($^1/_2$ becomes 0.5, $^3/_4$ becomes .75, etc.); then move the decimal one place to the right.

Any of these methods gives the dollar value for one bond at that price. If you are dealing with more than one bond, multiply again by the number of bonds involved.

Let's try this easy method for several different bond prices.

Example: What is the dollar value of one bond (1 M) selling at $88^3/_8$?

First, convert $88^3/_8$ to its decimal equivalent, and then move the decimal one place to the right: $88^3/_8$, in decimal form, is 88.375 Moving the decimal one place to the right makes the bond's dollar value $883.75.

There's no problem if you do not have the fractions memorized; you can always use your calculator to figure them.

CALCULATOR GUIDE

▶ 3 ÷ 8 = ◀ **0.375**

Then, instead of mentally moving the decimal, use the calculator to do it for you by multiplying by 10.

▶ 88.375 × 10 = ◀ **883.75** ($883.75)

Note that you can skip a whole step if you have the decimal equivalents for eighths memorized! If you know that $^3/_8$ equals 0.375, you multiply 88.375 by 10 (or move the decimal one place to the right) to find the dollar value for a single bond.

Example: What is the dollar value of 25 bonds (25 M) trading at 102^3/$_4$?

Since the fraction involved is an "easy" one, 102^3/$_4$ becomes 102.75.

Multiply 102.75 by 10 to get the dollar value of one bond: $1,027.50.

Multiplying again by 25 gives the dollar value for 25 bonds: $25,687.50

CALCULATOR GUIDE

▶ 3 ÷ 4 = ◀ **0.75**

Then

▶ 102.75 × 10 × 25 = ◀ **25,687.5** ($25,687.50)

Note that you can reduce the calculation to simply multiplying the value of a single bond (1,027.50) by 25 if you remember that one bond priced at 102^3/$_4$ is worth $1,027.50.

Premium, Par, and Discount

Bonds may trade at a *discount*, at *par*, or at a *premium*. Discount-priced bonds are valued at less than $1,000. When bonds are priced below 100 (94^1/$_4$, 97, 98^3/$_8$, etc.), they are said to be *trading at a discount* because they are priced at less than 100 percent of their face (par) value. When a discount price is converted to dollars, the answer is always less than $1,000! Therefore, if a $1,000 par bond is trading at less than 100 percent of its face value, it must be selling for less than $1,000.

Par-priced bonds are worth exactly $1,000. Bonds occasionally trade right at 100, that is, at 100 percent of their $1,000 par value, which is, of course, exactly $1,000. Such bonds are said to be *trading at par*. Most bonds are issued at, or very close to, par.

Premium-priced bonds have a value greater than $1,000. When bonds are priced above 100—such as 100^7/$_8$, 102, or 158^1/$_4$—they are said to be *trading at a premium*. Premium bonds are valued at more than $1,000 per bond.

Bond Pricing in the Secondary Market

Bond prices will vary from the time they are issued until the time they are redeemed. They are usually brought to market at or very close to par, and they mature at par. As interest rates change after a new bond is issued, its price in the secondary market will reflect such changes. If interest rates rise, the price of the bond will decline; if interest rates fall, the price of the bond will rise. Interest rates up, bond prices down. Interest rates down, bond prices up. This principle of *inverse proportionality* affects all fixed-income securities. A bond of a given quality (rating) and length to maturity will be offered to the public as a new issue at the then-current rate for such issues. If interest rates subsequently rise, other newly issued bonds will offer a greater return, making the older bond less attractive and causing it to decline in price. If, instead, interest rates subsequently decline, other newly issued bonds will offer a lower return than the older bond, making the older bond more attractive and causing it to trade at a higher price. As a bond's maturity date approaches, its price will get closer to par as investors realize that it will be redeemed at par in the relatively near future. Premiums and discounts thus will shrink as maturity approaches.

SELF-TEST

A. What is the dollar value of 10 M ABC bonds trading at $94^3/8$?

B. What is the dollar value of 100 M DEF bonds trading at $102^3/4$?

C. What is the dollar value of 1 MM GHI bonds trading at 100?

ANSWERS TO SELF-TEST

A. $9,437.50 [$94^3/8$ = 943.75, the value of one bond; then multiply by 10 for 10 bonds (10 M).]
These are *discount* bonds, so 10 bonds would be worth slightly less than $10,000.

B. $102,750.00 [$102^3/4$ = 1027.5, the value of one bond. Multiply by 100 for 100 bonds 100 M).]
These are *premium bonds,* so their market value will be greater than their par value (face value) of $100,000.

C. $1,000,000.00 (1 MM means $1,000,000 worth!)
This is equal to 1,000 $1,000 bonds. The dollar value of one bond at 100 would be $1,000. Multiply by 1,000 for a million dollars worth. These bonds are priced at *par,* so their market value is the same as their par value.

Chapter 3

PRICING GOVERNMENT BONDS AND NOTES

Generally considered to be the safest investments, U.S. government securities are very widely held by both individuals and institutions. They are "off the chart" with respect to their rating—higher than AAA—and have no risk with respect to defaulting on either principal or interest.

This text will not describe the nonmarketable government instruments—the *savings bonds*, Series EE, HH, and I—but will concentrate on the marketable issues, including bonds, notes, and bills. Government instruments are traded in much larger *blocks* than corporate and municipal bonds. A *round lot* of corporate bonds is considered to be $10,000 (10 M), and a round lot of government notes or bonds is $1 million (1 MM). These larger blocks necessitate a different pricing system for governments as opposed to corporate and municipal bonds.

Treasury Bond and Note Quotations

Among the debt instruments issued by the U.S. government are *Treasury notes*, with maturities from 1 to 10 years, and *Treasury bonds*, with maturities of more than 10 years. Like corporate bonds, Treasury notes and bonds are quoted as a percentage of their par value (see Chapter 2). The unit of trading for governments, however, is different from that for corporations. Treasury bonds and notes are traded in points and thirty-seconds of points rather than in points and eighths of points as are corporate bonds.

Why is that? Government notes and bonds normally trade in much larger blocks than corporate bonds—a round lot is $1 million (1 MM)! A one-eighth spread between the bid and ask prices for a block of $10,000 in corporate bonds (10 M) amounts to $12.50. A one-eighth spread on a $1 million worth of government bonds (1 MM) is $1,250!

Example: One-eighth on 10 (10 M) corporate bonds quoted 96 bid and offered at 96^1/$_8$ would be equal to $9,600 bid and $9,612.50 offered, a *spread* of only $12.50. That same eighth on $1 million worth (1 MM) of government bonds quoted at 96 bid and offered at 96^1/$_8$ would be equal to $960,000 bid and $961,250 offered, a spread of $1,250! This is too big a difference for trading purposes, so governments are traded in thirty-seconds to give traders more flexibility in negotiating prices.

There is one other small difference. Whereas corporate bond prices make use of fractions (such as 96^1/$_4$), government prices frequently make use of a colon to separate the whole number from the fraction.

Example: The quoted price for a government bond is 99:16. This means that the bond is trading for 99^{16}/$_{32}$ percent of its par value. That's correct, 99^{16}/$_{32}$ percent! The number following the colon (16) is the numerator for the fraction: 99:16 = 99^{16}/$_{32}$ percent. The denominator is always 32—only the numerator changes.

Treasury Bond and Note Dollar Equivalents

Treasury bonds and notes have face (or par) values of $1,000 (like corporate bonds). Government price computations are a little trickier than pricing corporate bonds, but the general principle is the same: Reduce any fraction to its decimal equivalent. To reduce the fraction to its decimal equivalent, simply divide the fraction's numerator (the top number) by its denominator (the bottom number). Move the decimal point one place to the right to get the dollar value of one bond.

Example: What is the price of a Treasury bond quoted at 99:24?

Reduce the fraction to its decimal equivalent. Divide the fraction's numerator (the top number, 24) by its denominator (the bottom number, 32):

99:24 = 99^{24}/$_{32}$ = 99^3/$_4$ = 99.75 (^{24}/$_{32}$ is equal to ^{3}/$_4$)

Move the decimal point one place to the right to get the dollar value of one bond:

$$99.75 = \$997.50 \text{ per bond}$$

If you have forgotten how to reduce fractions by the "least common denominator" system, use your calculator.

CALCULATOR GUIDE

▶ 24 ÷ 32 = ◀ **0.75**

Note: A corporate bond worth $997.50 would be quoted as 99³/₄, whereas a government bond worth that same dollar amount would be quoted as 99:24. It is important to remember this difference between corporate and government quotations: For T-bond or T-note quotations, everything to the right of the colon represents thirty-seconds!

Examples:

Corporate Bond Quote	Government Bond Quote	Dollar Value for One Bond
97¹/₈	97:04	$971.25
102¹/₄	102:08	$1,022.50
98³/₈	98:12	$983.75
110¹/₂	110:16	$1,105.00
96⁵/₈	96:20	$966.25
100³/₄	100:24	$1,007.50
99⁷/₈	99:28	$998.75

Any of the fractions can be reduced quite easily to decimal equivalents by dividing the number of thirty-seconds (the number after the colon) by 32.

Example: To calculate the dollar value of :17 (¹⁷/₃₂), divide 17 by 32.

$$17 \div 32 = \mathbf{0.53125}$$

Then move the decimal one place to the right: 0.53125 becomes 5.3125, or $5.3125. For a $1,000 bond, this is the dollar value of ¹⁷/₃₂.

Example: What is the dollar value of a government bond (1 M) trading at 99:16?

Reduce the quoted price to its decimal equivalent.

$$99:16 = 99^{16}/_{32} = 99.5$$

Then move the decimal one place to the right.

$$99.5 = 995. = \$995.00$$

The dollar price of one bond is $995.00.

CALCULATOR GUIDE

▶ 16 ÷ 32 = ◀ **0.5**

▶ 99.5 × 10 = ◀ **995.** ($995.00)

Note: Multiplying by 10 (as you just did in the "Calculator Guide") is the same as moving the decimal one place to the right. Multiplying by 100 moves the decimal point two places, multiplying by 1,000 moves the decimal three places, and so on. The decimal moves one place for each zero.

   Example: What is the dollar value of 100 M par value of government bonds trading at 102:08?

$$102:08 = 102^{8}/_{32} = 102.25$$

$$102.25 \times 10 = \$1,022.50$$

which is the value of one bond (1 M). Multiplying by 100 gives the value of 100 bonds (100 M):

$$100 \times \$1,022.50 = \$102,250.$$

Note: You can perform the same calculation by first moving the decimal one place to the right (thus multiplying by 10), which gives the one-bond value, and then moving the decimal two more places to the right, which gives the value for 100 bonds.

CALCULATOR GUIDE

▶ 8 ÷ 32 = ◀ **0.25**

Then

▶ 102.25 × 10 × 100 = ◀ **102250.** ($102,250.)

Note: You can skip the first step (dividing 8 by 32) if you know that ⁸/₃₂ is equal to ¹/₄. Then ¹/₄ becomes 0.25. You can then multiply 102.25 (102:08) first by 10 to get the one-bond value and then by 100 to get the 100-bond value!

Government Bond/Note Quotations

Price	Fraction	Decimal Equivalent	Dollar Value per Bond
:01	1/32	.03125	$0.3125
:02	2/32	.0625	$0.625
:03	3/32	.09375	$0.9375
:04	4/32	.125	$1.25
:05	5/32	.15625	$1.5625
:06	6/32	.1875	$1.875
:07	7/32	.21875	$2.1875
:08	8/32	.25	$2.50
:09	9/32	.28125	$2.8125
:10	10/32	.3125	$3.125
:11	11/32	.34375	$3.4375
:12	12/32	.375	$3.75
:13	13/32	.40625	$4.0625
:14	14/32	.4375	$4.375
:15	15/32	.46875	$4.6875
:16	16/32	.50	$5.00
:17	17/32	.53125	$5.3125
:18	18/32	.5625	$5.625
:19	19/32	.59375	$5.9375
:20	20/32	.625	$6.25
:21	21/32	.65625	$6.5625
:22	22/32	.6875	$6.875
:23	23/32	.71875	$7.1875
:24	24/32	.75	$7.50
:25	25/32	.78125	$7.8125
:26	26/32	.8125	$8.125
:27	27/32	.84375	$8.4375
:28	28/32	.875	$8.75
:29	29/32	.90625	$9.0625
:30	30/32	.9375	$9.375
:31	31/32	.96875	$9.6875

Chain Calculations

Sometimes it is necessary to reduce a series of government prices to dollar-and-cent amounts. This is when *chain*, or *consecutive*, *calculations* come into play. Most calculators are capable of doing chain calculations, thereby saving the user a lot of time. In the case of government bonds, you might need to divide many numerators by a single common denominator (32).

Note: In chain calculations, do not *clear the calculator after the first computation. Nor is it necessary to reenter the divide sign, the multiply sign, or the common figure in the chain. Your calculator also can do chain multiplication! Refer to "Chain Calculations" in the "How to Use the Calculator" section just before this book's Contents.*

Example: You are reducing several government bond fractions (such as $9/32$, $11/32$, $13/32$, and $15/32$) to decimal equivalents.

First, divide 9 by 32. After pressing the equals button ($=$), the calculator will show 0.28125, which is the decimal equivalent of $9/32$. *Without clearing the calculator,* enter 11 and then $=$. The calculator will now read 0.34375, the decimal equivalent of $11/32$. Note that you did not have to reenter the division sign ($\div$) or the denominator (32). Again, *without clearing the calculator,* enter 13 and then $=$. The calculator now shows 0.40625, the decimal equivalent of $13/32$. Now press 15 and then $=$, and the calculator will read 0.46875, the decimal equivalent of $15/32$.

CALCULATOR GUIDE

In chain division, you must record the answer to each calculation before entering the next numerator.

▶ 9 ÷ 32 = **0.28125**　　11 = **0.34375**　　13 = **0.40625**
15 = ◀ **0.46875**

Note: You did not have to reenter the division sign ($\div$) or the denominator (32).

SELF-TEST

A. What is the dollar value of 100 M U.S. Treasury $5 3/4$ percent notes due in 2018 and trading at 103:31?

B. What is the dollar value of 250 M U.S. Treasury $6 1/2$ percent notes due in 2019 and trading at 108:25?

C. What is the dollar value of 1 MM ($1 million) U.S. Treasury $5 1/4$ percent bonds due in 2029 and trading at 96:01?

ANSWERS TO SELF-TEST

A. $103,968.75   (1039.6875 × 100). The notes are trading at a premium (above par), so their market value is higher than their par value of $100,000.

B. $271,953.12   (1087.8125 × 250). Again, a premium-priced debt security with a market value higher than its par value of $250,000.

C. $960,312.50   (960.3125 × 1000). This bond is trading at a discount which will make its market value lower than its par value of $1,000,000.

PRACTICAL EXERCISE

➡ What would be the dollar value for each of the following Treasury notes?

1. 100 M at 103:16

2. 250 M at 97:08

3. 1 MM at 99:24

4. How would an investor be taxed on the *interest income* from such notes?

5. How would the investor be taxed on any *capital gain* resulting from the purchase and sale of these Treasury notes?

6. Might these issues of Treasury notes be callable?

Check your responses by referring to the "Answers to Practical Exercises" section after Chapter 26.

Chapter 4

DIVIDEND PAYMENTS

One of the *rights* of a common shareholder is the right to receive dividends—but only when, as, and if such dividends are declared by the corporation's board of directors. In recent years it has become less prevalent for corporations to pay dividends on their common stocks. During the great depression of the 1930s, approximately 33 percent of all publicly held corporations paid dividends; in 1978, dividends were paid by 67 percent of such corporations; and currently, less than 20 percent of common stocks pay dividends. One of the reasons advanced for this trend is that modern shareholders are more interested in growth (capital gains) than in income (dividends); another possible explanation is that corporations are loath to pay out dividends on common stocks because they are *not* deductible as a business expense, whereas shareholders are taxed—at regular rates—on such distributions. Some of the funds traditionally paid out as cash dividends are now used by corporations in "buy-back" programs.

All financially healthy preferred stocks and some common stocks pay dividends. These are usually cash payments. On occasion, corporations will pay stock dividends instead of cash dividends to their common shareholders, and some corporations pay common stockholders both cash and stock dividends.

A company's dividend policy—that is, the timing and amount of any dividends paid—is set by the board of directors. Most dividend-paying companies make cash distributions on a quarterly basis, paying dividends four times a year. This is not a legal requirement, and some companies pay out on other schedules. However, quarterly distributions definitely are the norm.

Most preferred stocks pay a fixed dividend, which is senior to any common stock dividends paid by that same company. These preferred dividends, while usually *fixed*, are not guaranteed. In times of financial stress, many corporations will suspend dividend payments on their preferred issues.

Ex-Dividend and Cum-Dividend Dates

To receive a forthcoming cash dividend, you must purchase the underlying stock, in the regular way, before the ex-dividend date. Persons buying the stock on or after the ex date will not receive the dividend.

The *Wall Street Journal* prints a "Corporate Dividend News" column each business day. It lists the dividends declared by various corporate boards of directors the previous day, as well as the stocks that will sell ex-dividend the following business day.

If you purchase a stock on or just after the ex-dividend date and thus do not receive the dividend, you do not necessarily suffer an economic loss. In theory, the stock will sell at a lower price on and just after the ex-dividend date to reflect the fact that the dividend is no longer attached to any stock now purchased. All other things being equal, the stock should sell lower by about the amount of the missing dividend.

> *Example:* If a stock is trading at 88.00 ($88 per share) and then goes ex for a $1 per share dividend, the stock most probably will trade at 87.00 ($87 per share) on the ex date. This, of course, presupposes that no other market forces are at play, such as a general rise or fall in the market or unusual buying or selling in that particular stock. In this instance, the stock will sell at 88.00 with the $1 dividend (cum dividend) and at 87.00 without the dividend (ex dividend).

Computing the Dollar Value of a Dividend

Holders are entitled to receive the stated rate for each share they own. To determine the total amount of the dividend to be received, multiply the per share amount of the dividend by the number of shares held.

> *Example:* An owner of 100 shares of a stock paying a per share dividend of $1.00 will receive a total of $100.00 (100 shares × $1.00 per share dividend); an owner of 325 shares will receive $325.00.

When a corporation has been paying regular quarterly dividends, future distributions usually continue at the same rate. If the company prospers, stockholders can anticipate a dividend increase, and the new regular quarterly rate will be set somewhat higher.

Note: Common stocks are not required to pay a certain dividend amount, and in fact, they are not bound to pay any dividend at all! While preferred stocks (with very few exceptions) have a fixed rate, common stocks do not.

Quarterly and Annual Dividend Rates

It is traditional to express a company's common stock dividend as "so much" per quarter. To arrive at the company's annual dividend rate, multiply the quarterly rate by 4.

> ***Example:*** If the current quarterly rate is $0.30, then the annual rate is $1.20: $0.30 × 4.

This calculation gives the anticipated dividend over the next year. Of course, the dividend could be raised, lowered, or even eliminated during that time. There is no absolute assurance that the owner of the stock will receive exactly this amount. The annual rate is only an *anticipated* rate.

> ***Example:*** Carlisle is listed as paying 1.28 annually ($1.28). A holder of 355 shares of Carlisle would receive $454.40 during the year.

▶ 355 × 1.28 = ◀ **454.4** ($454.40)

Who Gets the Dividend?

Here is the sequence of events for a dividend payment. The corporation's board of directors will meet to discuss the dividend. If the company is profitable, and especially if the company has had a record of paying dividends in the recent past, the board probably will authorize a cash dividend to be paid to the common stockholders.

The day the news is disclosed is known as the *declaration* date. The company announces the amount of the dividend, the *record date*, and the *payment* date. Soon thereafter, a fourth date, the *ex-dividend date*, is set by either a stock exchange or the National Association of Securities Dealers (NASD). This date, the ex date, falls between the declaration date and the record date. These four dates are, in chronological order: the declaration date, the ex-dividend date, the record date, and the payment date.

The declaration date is simply the date that the dividend announcement is made public. The details about the dividend, including the per-share amount, the ex date, the record date, and the payment date, will be printed in the financial press. Popular sources for such information include the *Wall Street Journal* and *Standard & Poor's Dividend Record*.

The ex-dividend date is *not* set by the corporation. It is set by the exchange on which the shares are traded if the stock is listed on a floor-based exchange or by the NASD for Nasdaq and over-the-counter stocks. The ex-dividend date is the first trading day that the stock trades *without* the dividend. If you are interested in receiving a forth-coming dividend, you must purchase the stock *before* the ex-dividend date (cum dividend). If you buy the stock on or after the ex date, you will *not* receive the dividend. The ex date is usually set 2 business days before the record date.

The record date is for the use of the dividend-disbursing agent. Whoever is listed as a shareholder at the close of business on the record date will receive the dividend. This is the deciding factor as to who gets the dividend: If you are listed as a shareholder at the close of business on the record date, then you will receive the dividend.

The payment date is the date that the shareholders actually will receive their dividend payments. Which shareholders? The shareholders who were listed on the transfer agent's books as of the close of business on the record date. This is the key: To receive a dividend, you must be listed on the transfer agent's books on the record date, and to be so listed, you must buy the stock *before* the ex-dividend date.

SELF-TEST

A. The CYA Corporation has an annual dividend rate of $0.88. How much will an owner of 350 shares of CYA receive each quarter?

B. If the CYA Corporation has a record date of Tuesday, June 13, what will be the ex date for the dividend?

C. What is the last day to buy CYA, in the regular way, so as to receive the dividend?

ANSWERS TO SELF-TEST

A. $77.00. An *annual* dividend rate of $0.88 means a *quarterly* rate of $0.22!

$$350 \times \$0.22 = \$77.00$$

B. Friday, June 9. The ex-dividend date is set 2 business days prior to the record date.

C. Thursday, June 8. You must purchase a stock *before* its ex-dividend date in order to receive a forthcoming dividend. Buying on June 8 means that you will be listed on the transfer agent's books on June 13, just in time to become a stockholder of record to receive the dividend.

PRACTICAL EXERCISE

▸ An investor wishes to purchase shares of Ambrosia, Inc. (traded on the New York Stock Exchange). The company's next cash dividend is payable to shareholders of record on Wednesday, July 15.

1. If the investor buys the stock, in the regular way, on Friday, July 10, when will he or she have to pay for the purchase?
2. Will this investor receive the forthcoming dividend?
3. What is the required holding period before the investor can sell the stock?
4. Who established the amount of the dividend?
5. Who set the ex-dividend date?
6. Who set the record date?

Check your responses by referring to the "Answers to Practical Exercises" section after Chapter 26.

Chapter 5

INTEREST PAYMENTS

Investors buy securities to "make money." The two ways that securities make money are through the generation of *income* and *capital gains*. Income is generated by stocks in the form of dividends (usually quarterly); income from bonds is generated by interest payments (usually semiannually). Many investors purchase stocks without regard to the dividends they may receive. They expect their reward to come in the form of a capital gain from "buying low and selling high." Other investors have income as their primary (or only) objective. Stocks may be bought for income or for a combination of income and capital gains, but usually bonds are bought only for income. While the value of bonds in the secondary market can fluctuate, generally in response to interest-rate changes, such changes are relatively minor compared with the extreme volatility experienced by the stock market.

While stocks pay dividends, bonds pay interest. A bond is not an equity (ownership) security, as are stocks, but rather a *debt* security. A bondholder does not own a "piece" of the business, like a stockholder, but simply has loaned money to the company. The bondholder thus has a creditor-debtor relationship with the corporation. When the bond matures, the bondholder will receive the principal (the *loaned*) amount—the face value—and interest payments will cease because the loan will have been repaid.

Semiannual Interest Payments

Until the bond matures, the company is expected to make regular interest payments on the loan. (There are some exceptions to this, notably with zero-coupon bonds.) While most stocks pay dividends quarterly (four times a year), most bonds make interest payments semiannually (twice a year). The months in which payments are made are indicated by the first letters of the months' names, and the months are always 6 months apart. The day of payment is indicated by a number following the second month's letter.

Examples: A bond's semiannual payments are indicated as "J & J1," which can only refer to January and July because they are exactly 6 months apart. June and July are only 1 month apart, and January and June are 5 months apart. Interest payments are made on the first day of each January and July.

"F & A15" indicates interest payments on the fifteenth of February and August (not February and April because they are only 2 months apart).

"M & N8" signifies interest payments due on the eighth of May and November. Can you figure out why "M & N" cannot mean *March* and November?

Most older bonds have interest payment dates of either the first or the fifteenth of the month, but more recently issued bonds tend to use a variety of dates.

The Dollar Value of Interest Payments

A bond's interest payment rate is usually shown either as a percent, such as "8.5%," or as "8¹/₂s." Both indicate that the bond has an interest rate of 8¹/₂ percent (8.50 percent) of its par value. A single bond (one bond, or 1 M) has a par value of $1,000, and for simplicity's sake, we will do almost all the calculations in the beginning part of this section using one bond as an example. (See Chapter 2, "Pricing Corporate Bonds," for a full explanation of a bond's par value.)

There are several ways to determine the amount of money that will be received, but probably the easiest is to

- Change the interest rate to its decimal equivalent.
- Move the decimal one place to the right. (This is the same method we used in Chapter 2 to change a bond's quoted price to its dollar equivalent.)

Example: A bond pays 8¹/₂ percent interest annually. To compute the amount of money that will be received over the year:

- Express the bond's interest rate in decimal format:

$$8^1/_2 = 8.5$$

- Move the decimal one place to the right: 8.5 becomes 85, or $85.

CALCULATOR GUIDE

Moving the decimal one place to the right is the same as multiplying by 10.

▶ 1 ÷ 2 = ◀ **0.5**

Then

▶ 8.5 × 10 = ◀ **85.** ($85.)

Example: A bond with an interest rate of 9³/₄ percent pays $97.50 annually.

Change 9³/₄ to 9.75, and then move the decimal one place to the right: $97.50.

CALCULATOR GUIDE

▶ 3 ÷ 4 = ◀ **0.75**

Then,

▶ 9.75 × 10 = ◀ **97.5** ($97.50)

Since two payments are made annually, each payment is one-half the annual amount.

Example: If a bond pays $85 in interest annually, one-half of this amount is paid every 6 months. The bondholder will receive two payments of $42.50 each, for a total of $85 over a year's time.

CALCULATOR GUIDE

▶ 85 ÷ 2 = ◀ **42.5** ($42.50)

Let's calculate bond interest on a more realistic number of bonds. Corporate bond round lots are 10 bonds ($10,000 par or face value). This number of bonds also can be shown as 10 M. To arrive at the dollar value of the interest payments on a block of bonds:

- Calculate the single-bond interest payment.
- Multiply the number of bonds by the single-bond interest payment.

Example: A block of 10 bonds (10 M, or $10,000 par value) with an interest rate of 11⁷/₈ percent pays total annual interest of $1,187.50.

- Calculate the annual single-bond interest payment. Change 11⁷/₈ to 11.875, and then move the decimal one place to the right. This effectively multiplies the number (11.875) by 10 and gives the annual interest for a single bond, $118.75.

- Multiply the annual single-bond interest payment ($118.75) by 10 (for 10 bonds) to arrive at $1,187.50.

CALCULATOR GUIDE

▶ 7 ÷ 8 = ◀ **0.875**

Then

▶ 11.875 × 10 × 10 = ◀ **1187.5** ($1,187.50)

An easier method of multiplying by 10 and then by 10 again is simply to move the decimal two places to the right. Thus 11.875, with the decimal moved two places to the right, becomes 1187.50, or $1,187.50.

Example: $100,000 worth (100 M) of $7^1/_4$ percent bonds pays total annual interest of $7,250.

Reduce $7^1/_4$ to 7.25, and then move the decimal three places to the right. This is equivalent to multiplying by 10 and then by 100! Thus 7.25, with the decimal moved three places to the right, becomes 7250.00, or $7,250.00.

This "move the decimal" method works well for 1 bond, 10 bonds, 100 bonds, or $1 million worth of bonds because you move the decimal 1, 2, 3, or 4 places, respectively.

CALCULATOR GUIDE

▶ 1 ÷ 4 = ◀ **0.25**

Then

▶ 7.25 × 10 × 100 = ◀ **7250.** ($7,250.)

Example: How much interest will be paid by a holding of 25 M $12^1/_8$ percent bonds?

First, convert the interest rate to a decimal. Thus $12^1/_8$ becomes 12.125. Multiplying by 10 and then by 25 gives interest of $3,031.25.

CALCULATOR GUIDE

▶ 1 ÷ 8 = ◀ **0.125**

Then

▶ 12.125 × 10 × 25 = ◀ **3031.25** ($3,031.25)

Have you learned to skip that first step yet? It saves a lot of time if you can start with 12.125 rather than having to divide 1 by 8. Come on, *memorize* these fractions:

$$^1/_8 = .125$$

$$^3/_8 = .375$$

$$^5/_8 = .625$$

$$^7/_8 = .875$$

Example: What annual interest will be paid on a position of 150 M 6⅝ percent bonds?

First, 6⅝ becomes 6.625. Multiplying by 10 and then by 150 gives total annual interest on the position of $9,937.50.

CALCULATOR GUIDE

▶ 5 ÷ 8 = ◀ **0.625**

Then

▶ 6.625 × 10 × 150 = ◀ **9937.5** ($9,937.50)

SELF-TEST

A. A "J & D" bond pays interest in which two months?

B. What amount of annual interest will be paid on 100 M 9 percent bonds?

C. What amount of annual interest will be paid on 1 MM 8⅜ percent bonds?

ANSWERS TO SELF-TEST

A. June and December (not *July* and December, which are only 5 months apart)

B. $9,000. [1 bond pays $90 per year; 100 bonds pay $9,000 (90 × 100)]

C. $83,750. [1 bond pays $83.75 per year; 1 M bonds pay $83,750 (83.75 × 1,000)]

PRACTICAL EXERCISE

▸ Mrs. Marianne Hynd has the following corporate bonds in her portfolio:

10 M ($10,000 par value) of ABC Corp. 6 percent at 107$\frac{1}{8}$

10 M ($10,000 par value) of DEF Corp. 5 percent at 103$\frac{1}{2}$

100 M ($100,000 par value) of GHI Corp. 8.5 percent at 97$\frac{3}{4}$

100 M ($100,000 par value) of JKL Corp. 10 percent at 120$\frac{5}{8}$

1. What is the *total* market value of her bond holdings?
2. What is the *total* amount of annual interest that Mrs. Hynd will receive from these bonds?
3. Should interest rates rise sharply, what effect might this have on the market value of Mrs. Hynd's bond portfolio?

Check your responses by referring to the "Answers to Practical Exercises" section after Chapter 26.

Chapter 6

ACCRUED INTEREST

This chapter will deal with a little-understood concept—accrued interest. It is important to understand the concept itself and the mathematics for calculating accrued interest. There are two different methods of figuration, one used for corporate and municipal bonds and another (more complicated) method used for government bonds.

When most bonds are purchased, in addition to the "cost" of the bond (its price as a percentage of its par value) and any commission, there will be another dollar figure on the client's confirmation, *accrued interest*. Interestingly, while the accrued-interest amount is added to the buyer's actual cost and the seller's actual proceeds, this amount is *not* included when reporting the bond's purchase cost or sales proceeds for tax purposes. The accrued interest is "backed out" by both buyer and seller (at least for tax reporting), with the seller adding the accrued interest he or she received to his or her other interest income for that tax year and the buyer subtracting the accrued interest he or she paid from his or her other interest income for that year. More on this in the "Practical Exercise" at the end of this chapter.

When stocks are purchased, they are bought either with the last declared dividend (cum dividend) or without it (ex dividend). Bonds do not work this way. With very few exceptions (such as zero-coupon bonds, adjustment bonds, and defaulted bonds), bonds trade *with accrued interest*.

Does this mean that if you sell a bond, you lose the interest earned on it since the last interest payment? No. When you sell a bond, you do not miss out entirely. You (the seller) and the buyer are each entitled to a portion of the next interest payment. You receive from the seller your fair share of the interest payment that will be made on the upcoming payment date, that is, the amount of interest that accrued to you while you owned the bond. You are due the interest earned while you owned the bond, and the buyer is entitled to the balance of that interest payment, the part representing the period that the purchaser will have owned the bond.

Settling Bond Trades

When does interest stop accruing to the seller and start accruing to the purchaser? In a transaction involving a corporate or municipal bond, the seller hands over the security sold and the buyer pays for the security bought on the settlement date. The seller is entitled to receive interest through the day before the trade settles. The buyer, who pays for the bond on the settlement date, starts collecting interest on that day. Thus the seller is entitled to receive accrued interest from the time he or she last received an interest payment through the day before settlement. This amount is paid to him or her by the buyer of the bond.

Example: On a J & J1 bond, interest payments are made on the first of January and the first of July (see Chapter 5, "Interest Payments"). If you own this bond and decide to sell it around the end of March, you last received an interest payment on the previous January 1. But you are also entitled to the interest accrued from the last interest payment you received (January 1) through the day before the transaction settles. This accrued interest will be paid to you by the buyer of the bond. The buyer, in turn, will receive the entire July 1 interest payment.

Most trades *settle* on the third business day after the trade date. This is true for stocks, corporate bonds, and municipal bonds and is known as *T+3 settlement.* (Options and government bonds settle on the first business day after the trade date, T+1.)

Example: If you buy a stock or corporate bond on Monday, the trade settles on the third business day thereafter, which is Thursday of that same week. Tuesday's trades settle on Friday of that same week, Wednesday's trades settle the following Monday, Thursday's trades settle the following Tuesday, and Friday's trades settle the following Wednesday.

When a legal holiday falls within the settlement period, the settlement day is moved one day forward.

Example: With a legal holiday falling on Wednesday, a Monday trade settles on Friday of that week rather than on Thursday.

Figuring Accrued Interest on Corporate and Municipal Bonds

You can calculate exactly how much accrued interest is due you. The formula for figuring accrued interest on a corporate or municipal bond trade is

Accrued interest = annual interest

$\times \dfrac{\text{number of days from last payment through day before settlement}}{360}$

Note: Accrued-interest calculations for corporate and municipal bonds use 360-day years and 30-day months.

Example: An 8 percent corporate bond is purchased, in the regular way, on Monday, January 5. How much accrued interest will be added to the purchase price? The bond pays interest on January 1 and July 1 (J & J1).

A corporate bond trade settles in 3 business days, so this trade will settle on Thursday, January 8. The seller last received interest on January 1, the previous interest payment day, and is entitled to interest from that day through January 7, the day before settlement. This means that the seller should receive 7 days' interest. A full year's interest on an 8 percent bond would be $80, and the seller "owned" the bond for 7 of the 360 days in the year. He or she is entitled to that percentage ($7/360$) of a full year's interest!

$$\$80 \times \tfrac{7}{360} = \tfrac{560}{360} = \$1.56$$

See how the formula was derived? This amount, $1.56 of accrued interest, will be paid by the buyer of the bond to the seller of the bond at settlement.

CALCULATOR GUIDE

▶ 80 × 7 ÷ 360 = ◀ **1.5555555** ($1.56)

Example: How much accrued interest will be added to a 10 M municipal bond traded on Wednesday,

November 10? The bond pays 7 percent interest and has payment dates of February 1 and August 1.

$$\$700 \times \tfrac{104}{360} = \$202.22$$

The interest payment date before the trade date was August 1. Accrued interest will be calculated from that date through November 14, the day *before* settlement day (trades on Wednesday, November 10, settle the following Monday, November 15). Accrued interest therefore includes all of August, September, and October—at 30 days each—and 14 days in November, a total of 104 days.

CALCULATOR GUIDE

▶ 70 × 10 × 104 ÷ 360 = ◀ **202.22222** ($202.22)

Note: We multiplied the annual interest on one 7 percent bond ($70) by 10 because we were dealing with 10 bonds (10 M).

Example: What amount of accrued interest would be added to a 250 M ($250,000) corporate bond trade executed on Friday, March 20? The bond has an interest rate of $9^{1}/_{2}$ percent and interest payment dates of A & O15.

$$\$23,750 \times \tfrac{160}{360} = \$10,555.56$$

This is a tricky one. First, did you know that A & O referred to April and October? We are using the *fifteenth* of those months as payment dates in our example, not the first. Since the trade date, March 20, was after October 15 but before April 15, we count accrued interest from October 15, the last payment date. It is easy to miscount the number of days for which interest is due in October. We "owe" interest from October 15 to the end of the month, keeping in mind that all months are considered to have 30 days. Count off the days—on your fingers, if necessary. There are *16* days from October 15 to October 30, inclusive. Since the trade date is Friday, March 20, the settlement date will be Wednesday, March 25. Accrued interest is owed for a total of 160 days, as follows:

Month	Number of Days of Accrued Interest	Remarks
October	16	October 15 through 30, *inclusive*
November	30	Use only 30-day full months
December	30	Use only 30-day full months
January	30	Use only 30-day full months
February	30	Use only 30-day full months
March	24	March 1 through March 24, the day before settlement
	160	Total days of accrued interest

CALCULATOR GUIDE

▶ 95 × 250 × 160 ÷ 360 = ◀ **10555.555** ($10,555.56)

Note: We multiplied the annual interest on one $9^{1}/_{2}$ percent bond ($95) by 250 because we were dealing with 250 bonds (250 M).

Figuring Accrued Interest on Government Bonds and Notes

Figuring accrued interest on U.S. government bonds and notes is a bit complicated. Since *governments*, as they are called, are traded in much larger blocks than municipal or corporate bonds ($1 million rather than $100,000 or $10,000), the accrued-interest calculation must be much more precise. The corporate/municipal rule of 30-day months and 360-day years is not used with governments. Actual days are used instead! Instead of using a full year's interest, we use only a half year's interest. This also means that we use only a half year of time instead of a full year. These differences make for much more precise, and fairer, accrued-interest calculations when dealing with the huge blocks of government bonds and notes that are traded.

Still another difference is that government note and bond trades settle on the next business day after the trade date. During nonholiday periods, Monday's trades settle on Tuesday of that same week, Tuesday's trades settle on Wednesday, and so on. Keep in mind that Friday's trades settle on the following Monday.

The government bond accrued-interest formula varies somewhat from the simpler formula used for corporates and municipals. For governments, we use one-half a year's interest and the number of days in the half year during which the trade took place.

The main things to remember are:

- Next business day settlement (T+1) rather than third business day settlement (T+3).

- *Actual* days in the month and year rather than 30-day months and 360-day years.

- One-half year's interest rather than a full year.

Example: A J & J1 government bond with a 6 percent interest rate will pay $60 annually in two $30 installments. There are two halves to the bond's "year"—the period from January 1 through June 30 (181 days) and the period from July 1 through December 31 (184 days). Assume a trade date of Wednesday, February 25 (in a non-leap year). The trade settles on Thursday, February 26, and accrued interest is figured through the day before settlement, or February 25. Since the trade took place in the January–July period (not July–January), we use 181 days as the denominator.

$$\$30 \times \tfrac{56}{181} = \$9.28$$

We owe accrued interest from the last interest payment before the trade, January 1, through the day before settlement. There are 31 days in January, and we accrue interest through February 25. Thus there are 56 days in the numerator (the number above the line). The denominator is the number of days in the entire half year from January 1 to June 30, that is, 181. January has 31 days; February, 28 (in a non-leap year); March, 31; April, 30; May, 31; and June, 30.

CALCULATOR GUIDE

▶ 30 × 56 ÷ 181 = ◀ **9.2817679** ($9.28)

Note: We used a half year's interest ($30). A 6 percent bond pays $60 annually, so a half year's interest is only $30.

Example: How much accrued interest will be added to a 200 M 8 percent government bond traded on Friday, August 3? The bond's interest-payment dates are M & N1.

The bond was traded in August, in the May–November half-year period (not November–May). Thus we must count the actual days in that period:

May	31
June	30
July	31
August	31
September	30
October	31
	184 This is the denominator in our formula.

Now we must figure which of the preceding interest days belong to the seller of the bond. The seller is entitled to accrued interest from May 1 (when he or she last collected interest) to the day before trade settlement. The Friday, August 3, trade settled on the Monday following (the next business day after the trade), August 6. The seller is therefore entitled to 5 days' interest in August—the number of days in that month through the day before settlement. Now we must count up the total number of days we owe the seller:

May	31
June	30
July	31
August	5
	97 The numerator in our formula.

Now that we have all the pieces, let's put it together. Keep in mind that we are dealing with 200 bonds.

$$\$8,000 \times \tfrac{97}{184} = \$4,217.39$$

CALCULATOR GUIDE

▶ 40 × 200 × 97 ÷ 184 = ◀ **4217.3913** ($4,217.39)

Note: An 8 percent bond pays $80 per year. We used a half year's interest, $40, and then multiplied by 200 because we were dealing with 200 bonds (200 M).

SELF-TEST

A. What amount of accrued interest will be added to a
trade of 10 M corporate 9 percent bonds sold on
Tuesday, March 12? Interest payment dates are
J & J1.

B. How much accrued interest will be paid by the
buyer of 125 M municipal bonds with a 6 percent
interest rate? The trade date is Thursday, April 10,
and interest payment dates are A & O1.

C. What amount of accrued interest is due on a trade of
50 M treasury bonds with a 7 percent interest rate
purchased on Wednesday, June 28. Interest payment
dates are M & N1.

ANSWERS TO SELF-TEST

A. $185.

▶ 900 × 74 ÷ 360 = ◀ **185.** ($185.)

Interest accrues from the interest payment date
preceding the trade, January 1, through the day
before settlement on Friday, March 15. Interest is
owed the seller for the full months of January and
February (at 30 days each) and 14 days in March, a
total of 74 days. For corporate and municipal bonds,
you must use 30-day months and 360-day years! A 9
percent bond pays $90 annually, so 10 bonds (10 M)
pay a total of $900.

B. $291.67

▶ 7500 × 14 ÷ 360 = ◀ **291.66666** ($291.67)

The interest payment dates are April and October 1,
and the trade settles on Tuesday, April 15. Only 14
days' interest is due because interest accrues through
the day *before* settlement. Again, corporate and
municipal bonds use 30-day months and 360-day
years. A 6 percent bond pays $60 annually;
therefore, 125 such bonds pay a total of $7,500
per year.

C. $561.14

▶ 1750 × 59 ÷ 184 = ◀ **561.1413** ($561.14)

Interest accrues through the day before settlement.
This is a government bond trade, so it settles on the
next business day, June 29. The day before
settlement is June 28, so many days in June are
owed, plus the complete month of May. We are

using actual days—half a year's interest—and half the total year as the denominator. The May 1 to November 1 half year has 184 days:

May	31
June	30
July	31
August	31
September	30
October	31
	184

Interest is owed from the previous interest payment before the trade, May 1, through the day before settlement on June 29:

May	31
June	28
	59

Because 7 percent bonds pay an annual total of $70, 50 M of these bonds pay an annual total of $3,500. We use one-half this amount, $1,750.

Note to Series 7 Preparatory Students

Hang in there. This section has covered the most difficult math on the examination. If you got this far and can do the arithmetic, you are well on your way to passing your licensing examination. The concept of accrued interest and the mathematics it involves can be formidable. It is important, however, in that it will be part of your job as a registered representative to be able to explain these concepts to customers. Reps may even be called on to prove out the accrued interest figures that appear on their clients' bond trade confirmations.

The series 7 examination probably will test the subject of accrued interest, but not exhaustively. You may be asked to figure actual accrued interest on small (1 M or 10 M) corporate or municipal bond trades, but most probably you will be tested only on the "actual days" and "next-day settlement" concepts with respect to government bond trades rather than a full-blown problem such as that in Question C of the Self-Test.

PRACTICAL EXERCISE

1. What amount of accrued interest will be added to a purchase of 10 M ($10,000 par value) of 7 percent corporate bonds purchased on Tuesday, November 18?

   The bonds are A & O1.

2. If the bond in Question 1 was purchased at 116¼ "net" by the client, what will be the total amount he or she must pay?

3. What will be the purchaser's tax-cost basis?

4. What amount of accrued interest will be added to a purchase of 1 MM ($1 million par value) of 5 percent Treasury bonds purchased on Monday, December 7?

   The bonds are F & A15.

Check your responses by referring to the "Answers to Practical Exercises" section after Chapter 26.

Chapter 7

CURRENT YIELD

Traditionally, when a dividend-paying stock is recommended by a brokerage, the write-up will include the stock's *current yield*. This chapter will explain what that yield is meant to tell the investor, how it is derived, and what its weakness is. It does little good for an investment to pay a handsome dividend and then fall dramatically in price. If somehow we were able to forecast the stock's future price movement, we could then come up with a much more meaningful statistic, *total return*.

Securities are purchased for investment. Presumably, investing properly will make your money grow—and will help your accumulated capital keep pace with, or even outstrip, inflation. Many investments are bought without regard for how much money they will bring in, on a regular basis, from dividends or interest. Instead, the investor hopes to have the market value of the investment grow over time so that the securities can be liquidated for a higher price than they were purchased for, that is, for *capital gains*. This "buy low, sell high" strategy is sometimes the only one employed, especially by very aggressive traders.

Other investors are concerned with regular income from their investments. Sometimes this is their only concern; sometimes they are striving for a combination of both benefits—capital gains and current income. In Chapters 7 through 10 we learn how to measure the continuing income from such investments.

Yield

The concept of *yield* is very important. Investors must be able to determine the amount of yield they receive and compare that yield with the returns (yields) available on alternate investments.

By analogy, farmland is valued in terms of its potential yield. The farmer understandably wants to know how large the harvests will be. The land must be prepared properly and the seed planted. Then a great deal of additional time and effort goes into weeding, watering, and protecting the crops from disease and the ravages of insects. It would be foolish for a farmer to even plant a crop without a fair degree of assurance that the money to be received from selling the crops will be sufficient to repay him or her adequately for all his or her time and trouble and the expense involved.

An investor also should be able to gauge the expected return from his or her investments. The *yield* on an investment gives the investor an idea of the return to be expected—what's in it for him or her. Such returns may be in the form of cash dividends (equity securities—common and preferred stocks) or interest payments (debt securities —bonds). He or she must then determine whether the expected return compares favorably with the yield that might be earned on alternate investments—and whether it is adequate enough to compensate him or her for the level of risk involved.

Yield is a measure of how much of the money the investor has risked will be returned to him or her each year in the form of dividends or interest. It shows the percent of the original investment that "returns" to him or her each year in cash.

Current Yield

One such measurement is known as *current yield*, which is derived by dividing an investment's current income by its current market price. By *current income*, we mean the amount of cash dividends the stock is expected to pay during the coming year. This calculation shows the percentage "return" for a purchaser of the stock at its current price—the percent of the purchase price that will be returned to the buyer over the coming year. The annual cash dividend is normally equal to four times the quarterly rate:

$$\text{Current yield} = \frac{\text{annual dividend}}{\text{current price}}$$

Example: XYZ common stock pays a quarterly dividend of $0.30 per share and is selling at 18.25 per share. What is XYZ's current yield?

$$\text{Current yield} = \frac{\$1.20}{18.25} = 6.58 \text{ percent}$$

CALCULATOR GUIDE

▶ .30 × 4 ÷ 18.25 × 100 = ◀ **6.57534** (6.58 percent)

Note: We had to multiply the quarterly dividend rate ($0.30) by 4 to arrive at the annual rate, $1.20. Note also that we added "× 100" as a last step to the equation. This permits us to read the percentage directly from the calculator window without the need for adjusting any decimals. Without this last step, the answer would show as "0.0657534" in the calculator window, and you would have to move the decimal two places to the right to change that number to a percentage. You can, of course, eliminate this last step simply by moving the decimal place two spaces to the right, but we'll stick with the "× 100" method for the balance of this text so that you can read the percentage answer directly from the calculator without moving decimals.

Thus, $1.20 is 6.58 percent of $18.25! It is the investor's return. He or she will receive in dividends, over the next year, 6.58 percent of the current price of the stock.

SELF-TEST

A. What is the current yield on a stock paying a quarterly dividend of $0.25 and trading at 24.89?

B. What is the current yield on a stock paying an annual dividend of $1.20 and trading at 45.55?

ANSWERS TO SELF-TEST

A. 4.02 percent

▶ .25 × 4 ÷ 24.89 × 100 = ◀ **4.01767** (4.02 percent)

Note that we had to multiply the quarterly dividend by 4 to arrive at the annual rate and that adding "× 100" to the formula allowed us to read the answer directly as a percent without moving any decimals.

B. 2.63 percent

▶ 1.20 ÷ 45.55 × 100 = ◀ **2.63446** (2.63 percent)

In this instance we were given the annual rate, $1.20, so there was no need to adjust it further.

Note: There are inherent weaknesses in the formula used to figure the current yield on common stocks. The numerator (the annual dividend) is at best an estimate of the total dividends per share that the common stock will pay over the next year. There is nothing certain about the amount of the common stock dividend. It is set by the company's board of directors, and the board might very well decide to raise, lower, or even eliminate the expected dividends. If the dividend is changed during the year, it will affect the stock's current yield.

Another weakness is that we do not know what the price of the stock will be 1 year from now! It might go up during that time—or down—and this too will affect the stockholder's return. We can eliminate one of these weaknesses—the uncertainty of the expected cash flow (dividends or interest) for the coming year—when dealing with fixed-income securities such as preferred stocks and bonds. The cash flow on such securities is consistent and is known in advance. There is no "guesswork" as to the amount of annual income that investments in these instruments will generate.

SELF-TEST

A. What is the current yield on a 9 percent bond trading at 104?

B. What is the current yield on a 6 percent bond trading at 94¹/₂?

ANSWERS TO SELF-TEST

A. 8.65 percent

▶ 90 ÷ 1040 × 100 = ◀ **8.65384** (8.65 percent)

A 9 percent bond pays interest of $90 per year. A bond priced at 104 has a dollar value of $1,040.

B. 6.35 percent

▶ 60 ÷ 945 × 100 = ◀ **6.3492** (6.35 percent)

A 6 percent bond pays interest of $60 per year. A bond priced at 94¹/₂ has a dollar value of $945.

Note: The 9 percent bond was selling at a premium. The bond's "nominal" yield (its interest rate) is 9.00 percent, but its current yield (8.65 percent) is somewhat less. The bond's current yield must be lower than the nominal yield. The only time a bond's nominal yield and its current yield are the same is when the bond is selling for exactly par (100).

Bonds trading at a premium always have a current yield that is less than their nominal yield, and bonds selling at a discount always have a current yield that is higher than their nominal yield. Note that the 6 percent bond in Question B is trading at a discount and that its current yield (6.35 percent) is higher than its nominal yield (6.00 percent).

The reason for this is fairly straightforward: A given bond pays a fixed rate of interest—so many dollars each year—whether it is trading in the open market at par, at a premium, or at a discount. The par buyer's nominal and current yield will be the same, but the "lucky" buyer who pays less than par will, of course, enjoy a better return. He or she is getting the same interest payments as the par buyer but paid less for the bond. By the same token, the buyer who paid more than par for the bond (a premium price) will not fare so well as the others because he or she "overpaid" for the bond. He or she receives the same interest as the others but paid more.

The higher the price paid for a given bond, the lower the yield.

NOMINAL YIELD

The concept of yield is quite important. Current yield and total return are measurements used for virtually all types of securities—both stocks and bonds—but nominal yield (the subject of this chapter) and yield to maturity (discussed in the two chapters following) apply exclusively to fixed-income securities.

With rare exception, bonds are bought for income—and thus the measurement of their income, and their yield, must be precise.

Coupon and Registered Bonds

Until the early 1980s, two types of bonds (particularly municipals) were issued—registered and coupon.

- *Registered bonds* have the owner's name, or the name of an institution holding the bonds for the owner, inscribed on them. The actual bondholder (the beneficial owner) is the true owner, whether the bonds are registered directly in his or her name or in an institution's name (*street name*). Currently issued bonds come only in the registered form, or as book-entry (described later).

- *Coupon bonds* (also known as *bearer bonds*) are not registered in any name. Like the dollar bills in your wallet, they are presumed to be the property of the person who has physical possession of them. The issuing corporation or municipality has no record of the actual owners—and, of course, has no way of paying the bonds' semiannual interest directly to these unknown holders. Interest is collected through the use of *coupons*. These coupons—one for each semiannual interest payment over the life of the bond—are attached to the bond certificate.

Every 6 months, coupon bondholders (or the institution holding the bonds for the owner) clip the appropriate coupon and present it to a bank for cash or deposit. A 30-year coupon bond had a total of 60 such coupons when first issued.

The expression *coupon clipper* refers to a person whose income is derived not from strenuous activity but from the rather pleasant task of simply cutting coupons from their bearer bonds and presenting them for payment. Coupon bonds have to be guarded very carefully because they (like dollar bills) are negotiable. When a coupon bond matures, all its coupons will have been detached, and the "body" of the bond certificate is then presented for repayment of its par value (redemption). When coupon bonds are traded, there is no need for the bonds to go through transfer because there is no owner's name on the bond, so there is no need to transfer from the name of the seller to the name of the buyer—the bonds are simply handed over to the new owner.

Coupon bonds have not been issued for some time, but the many outstanding coupon bonds have not been recalled. Such bonds will trade in the secondary market for another 10 years or so, and there are still plenty of them out there! These bonds were so prevalent in the past that the "street" still refers to interest payment dates as "coupon dates" and to the actual semiannual interest payments as "coupons."

> *Example:* A bond with an interest rate of 8 percent is referred to as an "8 percent coupon" bond.
>
> A J & J1 bond is said to have "coupon" payment dates of January and July 1.

For the balance of this text, we will refer both to a bond's coupon rate and its interest rate interchangeably—they both represent a bond's *nominal* yield.

Nominal Yield

A bond's coupon rate (its interest rate) is part of a bond's "name." As such, it is also called the *nominal yield*. The coupon rate is not influenced by either the bond's price or its maturity date; it simply refers to the bond's coupon (interest) rate.

> *Example:* "GM 9s of '19" describes a bond with an interest rate of 9 percent and a maturity date of 2019.

The 9 percent "coupon" rate—expressed to two decimal places as 9.00 percent—is the bond's nominal
yield. The GM 9s of '19 would have a nominal yield
of 9.00 percent whether they were trading at par, at a
premium, or at a discount. They would have a 9.00
percent nominal yield whether they were just 1 year or
20 years from maturity.

Knowing a bond's nominal yield enables you to determine the amount of interest paid by the bond. (See
Chapter 5 for the formula.)

SELF-TEST

A. What is the nominal yield on 6¹/₄ percent U.S.
Treasury bonds maturing in May of 2030 and
trading at 111:24?

B. Which has the greater effect on a bond's nominal
yield, its discount or its premium?

ANSWERS TO SELF-TEST

A. 6.25 percent. Bonds with a stated rate of interest of
6¹/₄ percent—whether they are corporate,
government, or municipal bonds—have a nominal
yield of 6.25 percent. Neither the fact that the issue
matures many years in the future nor its premium
price ($1,117.50 per bond) affects its nominal yield.

B. Neither has any effect. See the explanation for the
preceding question.

*Note: Keep in mind that nominal yield is just an exotic way of
expressing a bond's stated interest rate, its coupon rate.*

Chapter 9

YIELD TO MATURITY: BASIS PRICING

Professional investors (mutual funds, insurance companies, pension funds, banks) are high-volume buyers of debt securities. They ordinarily purchase these fixed-income securities for the longer term—often buying them with no intention to sell, merely to hold them until they mature. They buy and sell bonds not on a *dollar* basis (as do most individuals) but on a *yield* basis. A pension fund interested in adding a half-million dollars of par value of the POS Corporation's bonds to its fixed-income portfolio is not particularly interested in the bond's market price! The fund does not really care whether it pays $240,000 for the bonds, or $250,000, or even $260,000— what it wants to know is, "If we buy these bonds and hold them until they mature, what will our return be?" The price itself is not material because the *basis* (explained later) takes everything into account—the price, the coupon rate, and the length to maturity. It is a very sophisticated way to measure yield.

The most professional measurement of a bond's return is its *yield to maturity*. This is a rather complicated concept involving a bond's total return if it is held until it matures. It takes into account the purchase price of the bond, its redemption value, the coupon rate, and the length of time remaining to the bond's maturity. Yield to maturity utilizes the concept of present value and assumes that all coupons are reinvested at the yield-to-maturity rate. This is also known as the *internal rate of return*.

Confused? In plainer English, yield to maturity is the truest measure of the return that a bond investor would receive by holding the bond until it matures. Under these conditions, all cash inflows (the interest payments during the life of the bond and the principal payment at maturity) and expenses (the cost of the bond) can be precisely calculated in advance. Since we are dealing with a fixed-income security, there is no uncertainty about the amount of income to be received (as there would be with a common stock). And the ultimate "sale" price for the security (the return of principal) is also known; if the bond is held until maturity, the issuing corporation will redeem it at par, $1,000. Isn't this the same, in financial terms, as simply "selling" the bond at par?

This yield calculation also factors in the difference between the par value of the bond and its purchase price. For example, if you pay less than par for a bond and hold it to maturity, you will then receive a full $1,000; the yield-to-maturity figures in these additional funds (the discount). If you pay a premium price for a bond—more than the par value you will receive at maturity—this "loss" is also taken into account (the premium).

When figuring nominal yield, we look at the bond's stated rate of interest but ignore the bond's price and its maturity date. When figuring current yield, we factor in the bond's price and nominal yield but disregard the length of time to maturity. When dealing with yield to maturity, we factor in all these elements.

We know:

- The bond's nominal yield
- The price of the bond—its current price—and any premium or discount
- The amount of interest that will be received
- The "sale" price—full par value at maturity ($1,000 per bond)

Factoring in all these elements, using present values and even accounting for the reinvestment of interest payments as they are received, gives us yield to maturity, the most professional way of figuring yield on long-term debt instruments.

Example: While bonds are sometimes quoted as a percentage of par, such as 98$^{1}/_{2}$ or 102$^{3}/_{4}$, most professionals quote bonds, especially municipals, on a "yield" basis—at the bond's yield to maturity. As we shall soon explain, a 10-year 9 percent bond trading at 96 also can be quoted on a 9.63 "basis." This means that a bond with a 9 percent coupon trading at a current price of 96 ($960) and maturing in 10 years has a yield to maturity of 9.63 percent.

How, then, is yield to maturity computed? There are several ways to determine a bond's true yield to maturity.

This chapter demonstrates the use of the yield basis book. Chapter 10 shows the rule-of-thumb method.

The Yield Basis Book

The most commonly employed methods for calculating yield to maturity include using either a *yield basis book* or a programmable calculator. A simplified page from a basis book is reproduced below. Most basis books are a lot more detailed than this sample page. They would be in increments of single or half years (or even months) rather than 5 years, and the price column might be in half-point increments or less rather than the 2-points increments illustrated. But the page as shown is more than adequate for our purposes.

Sample Page from a Bond Yield Basis Book

	9 Percent Coupon		
Price	*Years to Maturity*		
	5	**10**	**15**	**20**
92.00	11.13	10.30	10.04	9.93
94.00	10.58	9.96	9.77	9.68
96.00	10.04	9.63	9.51	9.45
98.00	9.51	9.31	9.25	9.22
100.00	9.00	9.00	9.00	9.00
102.00	8.50	8.70	8.76	8.79
104.00	8.01	8.40	8.52	8.58
106.00	7.54	8.11	8.29	8.38
108.00	7.07	7.83	8.07	8.18

This table would be used for bonds with a 9.00 percent nominal yield (a 9 percent coupon) priced in the range from 92 to 108 with maturities from 5 to 20 years. An actual yield book would have different pages for other coupon rates such as 8⁷/₈ percent and 9¹/₈ percent, and each page would include many more figures than our sample.

A basis book may be used to convert a bond's price to its yield to maturity—or its yield to maturity to a price. A bond's price is a dollar amount, expressed as a percentage of the bond's par value. A bond priced at 98¹/₄ would sell for $982.50; a bond quoted at a price of 103³/₈ would be worth $1,033.75. A bond's yield to maturity is a percent.

(See Chapter 2 for bond pricing.) A bond with a 7.58 *basis* has a yield to maturity of 7.58 percent.

Converting Price to Yield to Maturity

Example: What is the yield to maturity for a 10-year bond with a 9 percent coupon offered at 94? In the preceding table, locate the bond's price in the first column, and then read across that line two places to the right. Now you are looking at the intersection of the 94.00 price line and the 10 years time-to-maturity line. This intersection reads "9.96," which is the bond's yield to maturity, 9.96 percent. An investor paying 94 ($940) for the bond and holding it until it matures would have a yield to maturity on his or her investment of 9.96 percent. Note that the bond is trading at a discount; thus its yield to maturity (as well as its current yield) will be higher than its nominal yield.

- This bond's nominal yield (its coupon rate) is 9.00 percent.
- This bond's current yield is 9.57 percent ($90 ÷ 940 = 9.57 percent).

CALCULATOR GUIDE

▶ 90 ÷ 940 × 100 = ◀ **9.57446** (9.57 percent)

This bond's yield to maturity is 9.96 percent (from the yield table).

The current yield is higher than the nominal yield because you are factoring in the relatively low price (a discount) you paid for the bond in return for the interest payments. The yield to maturity is higher yet because you are also taking into account the fact that more money will be repaid to the buyer at maturity ($1,000) than was paid for the bond ($940).

Example: What is the yield to maturity for a 20-year 9 percent bond priced at 106? In the sample yield table, read down the price column until you hit 106.00. Then scan over four columns to the right (the 20 years column) to a yield to maturity of 8.38 percent. An investor paying 106 ($1,060) for the bond and holding it until it matures would have a yield to maturity on his or her investment of 8.38 percent. Since the bond is trading at a premium, both its current yield and its yield to maturity will be below its nominal yield.

- This bond's nominal yield is 9.00 percent (its coupon rate).
- This bond's current yield is 8.49 percent ($90 ÷ 1,060 = 8.49 percent).

CALCULATOR GUIDE

▶ 90 ÷ 1060 × 100 = ◀ **8.49056** (8.49 percent)

This bond's yield to maturity is 8.38 percent (from the yield table).

Since we are dealing with a bond selling at a premium, we know that both its current yield and its yield to maturity will be lower than its nominal yield. The current yield is lower than the coupon rate (nominal yield) because the bond was bought for greater than its par value. The yield to maturity is still lower, reflecting the fact that the investor will pay $1,060 for the bond but will only get back $1,000 when the bond matures.

Converting Yield to Maturity to Price

Example: What is the price of a 9 percent 15-year bond selling at a 9.51 basis? Using the sample basis table, run down the 15 years column until you hit the 9.51 figure. Then scan to the left, all the way to the price column, and find the price of 96.00. The price for a 9.51 basis bond is 96.00, which, expressed in dollars, comes to $960 per bond.

Note that the basis, 9.51, is higher than the coupon rate. This indicates that the 9 percent bond must be selling at a discount. If a buyer earns more than the coupon rate, he or she is buying the bond for less than its par value.

Example: What is the price for a 9 percent 5-year bond selling at a 7.07 basis? Using the same table, go down the 5 years column until you hit the 7.07 figure. Then scan all the way to the left to find the price of 108. This price equals $1,080 per bond, a premium price. Since a buyer would have to pay more than par to buy this bond, he or she would receive a yield of less than the coupon rate.

Note: The yield shown for Treasury bonds and notes in the newspaper listings (in the "Ask Yld." column) is yield to maturity.

The yield shown in the newspaper listings for corporate bonds is current yield. Many municipal bonds, especially serial bonds, are quoted on a yield basis rather than at specific dollar prices. That yield basis is yield to maturity. More on this in Chapter 11.

Interpolating the Yield Basis Book

The basis book works fine when you are converting a price to a yield and the exact bond price is listed in the table. But what do you do when the price is not listed? This is when you must interpolate. *Interpolation* is the method of estimating an unknown number that is between two known numbers.

Let's use a little piece of the table we have been practicing on. We can see immediately that a 9 percent 10-year bond priced at 94.00 has a yield to maturity of 9.96 percent and that a 9 percent 10-year bond priced at 96.00 has a yield to maturity of 9.63 percent.

| | 9 percent Coupon |
Price	*10 Years*
94.00	9.96
96.00	9.63

But what about a bond priced at 95.00? The 95 price is exactly halfway (50 percent of the way) between the prices of 94 and 96. Thus we assume that the yield to maturity for a bond at that price will be halfway (50 percent of the way) between the 9.96 and 9.63 basis prices. There is a difference of .33 between 9.96 and 9.63 (9.96 − 9.63 = .33). Fifty percent of that difference is 0.165 (0.5 × 0.33).

Note that as the prices go up, the yields go down. Therefore, we have to *lower* the 9.96 basis price by 0.165, reducing it to 9.465 (9.96 − .165 = 9.795). This gives us the yield to maturity for a 9 percent 10-year bond priced at 95, a 9.795 basis.

To solve more difficult examples, it is necessary to establish a proportion. A proportion is an equality between ratios. These are fairly simple to do.

Example: In the preceding example, we would say that "1 is to 2 as *x* is to .33." The *x* is what we are look-

ing for, the amount we have to subtract from the 9.96
yield for a bond trading at 94 to arrive at the yield for
a bond trading at 95.

Let's identify all the figures used in the computation:

- 1 is the difference between the 94 and 95 bond prices.
- 2 is the difference between the 94 and 96 prices.
- The unknown quantity (x) is the difference between
  the 9.96 yield and the figure we are seeking.
- .33 is the entire difference between 9.96 and 9.63.

To solve the problem, we multiply the "outside"
numbers (1 × .33) and then divide by the known
"inside" number (2).

$$(1 \times .33) \div 2 = 0.165$$

CALCULATOR GUIDE

▶ 1 × .33 ÷ 2 = ◀ **0.165**

We then subtract the figure derived, 0.165, from 9.96 to
arrive at our answer of 9.785. This is the yield to maturity
for a bond priced at 95.00.

SELF-TEST

Use the yield book table to answer the following questions:

A. What is the yield to maturity for a 15-year 9 percent
bond trading at 98?

B. What is the yield to maturity for a 10-year 9 percent
bond trading at par?

C. What is the yield to maturity for a 5-year 9 percent
bond trading at 103?

D. What is the yield to maturity for a 20-year 9 percent
bond trading at 104^1/$_2$?

ANSWERS TO SELF-TEST

A. 9.25 percent. Go down the 15 years column and
across the 98.00 line and read the answer where the
lines intersect: 9.25.

B. 9.00 percent. We really do not need the table to
solve this one because bonds trading at par (100)
have a current yield and a yield to maturity that is

exactly equal to their nominal yield. But check it out
on the table anyway. Go down the 10 years column
until it intersects with the 100.00 line. There's the
answer: 9.00 percent.

C. 8.26 percent. The precise answer is 8.255 percent,
which can be rounded off to 8.26 percent. The
answer can be "eyeballed" if you realize that the
yield you are looking for is halfway between the 102
and 104 prices, and therefore, the answer is to be
found halfway between their respective yields. The
halfway point between 8.50 and 8.01 is 8.255 (8.50
+ 8.01 ÷ 2 = 8.255).

But let's also solve this one the "proper" way by
setting up a proportion. (This is what you have to do
when dealing with more complex problems anyway.)
The proportion sets up this way:

1 is to 2 as x is to .49

- 1 is the difference between the 102 price and the price
  we are looking for, 103.
- 2 is the difference between the two prices on either
  side of the price we are seeking, 102 and 104.
- x is the figure we must subtract from the 8.50 yield to
  reduce it to the yield for a 103 price.
- .49 is the difference between 8.50 and 8.01, the yields
  on either side of the yield we are looking for.

To solve, we multiply the two outside numbers and
divide by the known inside number. The outside
numbers in the proportion are 1 and .49. The
known inside number is 2, so we multiply 1 and .49
and then divide by 2.

▶ $1 \times .49 \div 2 =$ ◀ **0.245**

This is the amount we must subtract from the 8.50
yield to arrive at the yield for a bond priced at 103.
That is, 8.50 − 0.245 = 8.255.

D. 8.53 percent. Here's the proportion:

.50 is to 2 as x is to .20.

Multiplying the outside numbers and then dividing by the known inside number gives 0.05 (.50 × .20 ÷ 2 = 0.05). We then subtract that number from 8.58: 8.58 − 0.05 = 8.53.

If you did not follow the explanation, here is where all the numbers came from:

- The prices bracketing the price we are seeking are 104 and 106. The difference between these two numbers is 2.
- The difference between the first price, 104, and the price we are looking for, 104.50, is .50.
- The difference between the yields for 104 and 106 is .20 (8.58–8.38).

Note: This is very esoteric stuff and not easily mastered. While you should know the general principles of interpolation, you can take comfort in the fact that a detailed basis book makes most interpolation unnecessary—and using a programmable calculator completely eliminates all these hand calculations.

PRACTICAL EXERCISE

▸▸ Use the following bond yield table to answer all questions.

▸▸ Calculate *yields* to two decimal places (8.82 percent, 11.03 percent).

▸▸ Calculate bond *prices* to the nearest cent ($1,009.63, $991.88).

1. What is the yield to maturity for a 10³/₄ percent bond maturing in 11 years that is trading at 96.50?

2. What is the price of a 10³/₄ percent bond maturing in 10 years that is being offered on a 10.67 basis?

3. What is the yield to maturity for a 10³/₄ percent bond maturing in 9¹/₂ years that is trading at 109.00?

4. What is the price of a 10³/₄ percent bond maturing in 12 years that is being offered on an 11.17 basis?

Check your responses by referring to the "Answers to Practical Exercises" section after Chapter 26.

10 3/4 Percent			Years to Maturity			
Price	8	9	10	11	12	13
96.00	11.53	11.47	11.43	11.40	11.37	11.35
96.50	11.43	11.38	11.34	11.31	11.29	11.27
97.00	11.33	11.29	11.26	11.23	11.21	11.19
97.50	11.23	11.20	11.17	11.15	11.13	11.12
98.00	11.13	11.11	11.09	11.07	11.05	11.04
98.50	11.04	11.02	11.00	10.99	10.98	10.97
99.00	10.94	10.93	10.92	10.91	10.90	10.90
99.50	10.85	10.84	10.83	10.83	10.83	10.82
100.00	10.75	10.75	10.75	10.75	10.75	10.75
100.50	10.66	10.66	10.67	10.67	10.68	10.68
101.00	10.56	10.58	10.59	10.59	10.60	10.61
102.00	10.38	10.40	10.42	10.44	10.45	10.47
103.00	10.19	10.23	10.26	10.29	10.31	10.33
104.00	10.01	10.06	10.11	10.14	10.17	10.19
105.00	9.83	9.90	9.95	9.99	10.02	10.05
106.00	9.66	9.73	9.80	9.84	9.89	9.92
107.00	9.48	9.57	9.64	9.70	9.75	9.79
108.00	9.31	9.41	9.49	9.56	9.61	9.66
109.00	9.14	9.25	9.35	9.42	9.48	9.53
110.00	8.97	9.10	9.20	9.28	9.35	9.40

Chapter 10

THE RULE-OF-THUMB YIELD TO MATURITY

Want an interesting exercise? After finishing this chapter, go back to Chapter 9 and look up several yields to maturity on the 10 3/4 percent basis book page illustrated in the "Practical Exercise." Note their dollar prices. Now do a rule-of-thumb yield to maturity for those dollar prices and compare your yield answers to the basis book answers. It will give you an appreciation of how close (or how far away) yields to maturity are when looked up in a basis book as compared with a rule-of-thumb calculation. If you have access to an HP12c (or equivalent) calculator, run those same figures (the coupon, price, and length to maturity) through. You should come up with exactly the same yields as when using the basis book.

The yields in Chapter 9's sample basis book page are the same as the yields that would be obtained through the use of a calculator programmed for the figuration of such yields. But what if you are trying to figure a yield to maturity and you do not have a basis book or a properly programmed calculator at hand? You can arrive at an *approximation* of a bond's yield to maturity through the rule-of-thumb method. This may be sufficient for your purposes, but keep in mind that the yield obtained is at best an approximation. It is not the exact yield to maturity but merely "in the ballpark." One should use either a bond calculator or the basis book if available; the rule-of-thumb method should be used only when you are "out in the field" and do not have the proper tools available!

The Formula

The formula for the rule-of-thumb yield to maturity is a variation of the current yield formula. For bonds trading at a discount (priced less than 100), the formula is

$$\text{Rule-of-thumb yield to maturity} = \frac{\text{annual interest} + (\text{discount} \div \text{years to maturity})}{(\text{current price} + \text{par}) \div 2}$$

For bonds trading at a premium (priced more than 100), the formula is

$$\text{Rule-of-thumb yield to maturity} = \frac{\text{annual interest} - (\text{premium} \div \text{years to maturity})}{(\text{current price} + \text{par}) \div 2}$$

Notice that the numerator takes into account that the bond might be purchased at either a discount or a premium. Since all bonds are redeemed at par when they mature, the calculation takes into account

- Either the "extra" money that eventually will be earned by the bondholder if he or she buys the bond at a discount, because he or she purchased for less than par but will receive par at maturity.
- Or the money that will be lost when a bond is bought at a premium, because he or she purchased for more than par but will only receive par at maturity.

This profit or loss is "spread" over the years to maturity as an addition to or a subtraction from the interest payments. This makes sense.

- An investor buying a bond at a discount (below 100) has two sources of income: the semiannual interest payments and the additional income that he or she eventually will receive (the difference between the purchase price of less than $1,000 per bond and the $1,000 the issuer will pay when the bond matures).
- The investor buying a bond at a premium (above 100) eventually will suffer a loss when the bond matures. Having paid more than par for the bond, he or she will receive only $1,000 from the issuer at maturity. This is why we subtract the premium from the interest payments; it reflects that loss.

Therefore, in the numerator (the numbers above the fraction line)

- Any discount earned, annualized, is *added* to the annual interest.

- Any premium, annualized, is *subtracted* from the annual interest.

Note: Annualized *means spread out over the years to maturity. We annualize by dividing the premium or discount by the number of years to maturity. This is why, in the formula, the discount or premium is divided by the number of years to maturity.*

The denominator, taken from the current yield formula, is changed in that we use the *average* of the current price and the bond's value at maturity (always $1,000). This is why the two values are added together and divided by 2; this gives us an *average* of the current price and the value at maturity.

Bonds at Discount Prices

Example: What is the rule-of-thumb yield to maturity for a 7 percent 10-year bond trading at 94?

Applying the first of the two formulas shown earlier (for discount bonds):

Rule-of-thumb yield to maturity

$$= \frac{\$70 + (\$60 \div 10)}{(\$940 + \$1,000) \div 2} = \frac{\$70 + \$6}{\$1,940 \div 2}$$

$$= \frac{\$76}{\$970} = 7.84 \; percent$$

CALCULATOR GUIDE

If you are comfortable with the conversion of a bond's price and coupon rate into dollars, use this calculator guide.

▶ 940 + 1000 ÷ 2 M+ 60 ÷ 10 + 70 ÷ Mrc × 100 = ◀
7.83505 (7.84 percent)

Note: M+ indicates the memory-plus button on the calculator. Mrc indicates the memory-recall button.

- 940 is the bond's quoted price (94), expressed in dollars.

- 1,000 is the bond's value at maturity (par).
- 60 is the dollar difference between the cost of the bond and its redemption value (1,000 − 940).
- 10 is the number of years to maturity.
- 70 is the annual interest rate (7 percent), in dollars.

Here's another method. You may find it useful if you are not comfortable converting bond price and coupon rates into dollars.

CALCULATOR GUIDE (ALTERNATE METHOD)

▶ 100 + 94 ÷ 200 M+ 100 − 94 ÷ 10 + 7 ÷ Mrc = ◀
7.8350515 (7.84 percent)

Note: M+ indicates the memory-plus button on the calculator. Mrc indicates the memory-recall button.

With this method, it is unnecessary to change a bond's quoted price or coupon rate into dollar equivalents. Here is where the numbers came from:

- 100—this is a constant in this method—is the "price" of the bond at maturity.
- 94 is the bond's current price (had the bond been priced at 88½, this figure would have been 88.5).
- 200 is a constant in this method.
- 100 is a constant.
- 94 is the bond's current price.
- 10 is the number of years to maturity.
- 7 is the bond's coupon (interest) rate. As with the bond's price, any fraction in the coupon rate should be expressed as a decimal.

Bonds at Premium Prices

The preceding example used a bond selling at a discount. The amount of the annualized discount was added to the interest income. The next example uses a premium bond, and we will have to *subtract* the annualized premium from the interest income.

Example: What is the rule-of-thumb yield to maturity for a 9½ percent 12-year bond selling at 106?

Rule-of-thumb yield to maturity

$$= \frac{\$95 - (\$60 \div 12)}{(\$1,060 + \$1,000) \div 2} = \frac{\$95 - \$5}{\$2,060 \div 2}$$

$$= \frac{\$90}{\$1,030} = 8.74 \; percent$$

CALCULATOR GUIDE

▶ 1060 + 1000 ÷ 2 M+ 60 ÷ 12 = +/− + 95 ÷ Mrc ×
100 = ◀ **8.73786** (8.74 percent)

Note: +/− indicates the calculator's reverse-sign key. If your calculator lacks such a key, use the following method.

CALCULATOR GUIDE (FOR CALCULATORS LACKING A REVERSE-SIGN KEY)

▶ 1060 + 1000 ÷ 2 M+ 60 ÷ 12 = (5.) (Either remember
this number or write it down.)

on/c 95 − 5 ÷ Mrc × 100 = ◀ **8.73786** (8.74 percent)

After dividing by 12 and pressing the equals (=) button, the calculator window shows "5." You must remember this number, or write it down—we show it as (5.)—and then subtract it from the bond's coupon rate (95 − 5) after you clear the calculator's last entry by pressing "on/c." This extra step is necessary when working with a premium-priced bond and you are using a calculator without a reverse-sign (+/−) key.

SELF-TEST

A. What is the rule-of-thumb yield to maturity for a 20-year bond with a 12 percent coupon trading at 96?

B. What is the rule-of-thumb yield to maturity for a bond with a 7 percent coupon rate, 10 years to maturity, and a price of 107$^{1/4}$?

ANSWERS TO SELF-TEST

A. 12.45 percent. A 12 percent bond pays annual interest of $120. The price of 96 ($960) represents a

$40 discount, which, annualized over 20 years, adds $2 to the numerator. A 12 percent bond trading at a discount must have a current yield and a yield to maturity greater than its coupon rate.

$$\frac{\$120 + (\$40 \div 20)}{(\$960 + \$1,000) \div 2} = \frac{\$120 + \$2}{\$1,960 \div 2}$$

$$= \frac{\$122}{\$980} = 12.45 \text{ percent}$$

CALCULATOR GUIDE

▶ 960 + 1000 ÷ 2 M+ 40 ÷ 20 + 120 ÷ Mrc × 100 = ◀
12.44897 (12.45 percent)

CALCULATOR GUIDE (ALTERNATE METHOD)

▶ 100 + 96 ÷ 200 M+ 100 − 96 ÷ 20 + 12 ÷ Mrc = ◀
12.448979 (12.45 percent)

- 96 is the bond's price.
- 20 represents the years to maturity.
- 12 is the coupon rate.

B. 6.06 percent. A 7 percent bond pays $70 in annual interest. The price of 107¼ ($1,072.50) represents a $72.50 premium, which, annualized over 10 years, subtracts $7.25 from the numerator. Since the bond is trading at a premium, it is to be expected that the yield to maturity will be below the bond's coupon rate.

$$\frac{\$70 - (\$72.50 \div 10)}{(\$1,072.50 + \$1,000) \div 2} = \frac{\$70 - \$7.25}{\$2,072.50 \div 2}$$

$$= \frac{\$62.75}{\$1,036.25} = 6.06 \text{ percent}$$

CALCULATOR GUIDE (FOR CALCULATORS EQUIPPED WITH A REVERSE-SIGN KEY)

▶ 1072.50 + 1000 ÷ 2 M+ 72.50 ÷ 10 = +/− + 70 ÷
Mrc × 100 = ◀ **6.05548** (6.06 percent)

CALCULATOR GUIDE (ALTERNATE METHOD)

▶ 100 + 107.25 ÷ 200 M+ 100 − 107.25 ÷ 10 + 7 ÷
Mrc = ◀ **6.0554885** (6.06 percent)

With this alternate method you enter the bond's current value as a price (107.25) rather than as a dollar value ($1,072.50), and you enter the interest rate as a percent (7) rather than a dollar value ($70).

PRACTICAL EXERCISE

▸ Fortuna Corporation 8 percent bonds are trading at 96$^1/_2$. They are due to mature in 10 years and are currently callable at 102$^3/_4$.

1. What is the current yield on the Fortuna bonds?
2. What is the rule-of-thumb yield to maturity on these bonds?
3. Will the yield to call be greater or less than the yield to maturity?

▸ Natacomb Corporation 6 percent bonds are trading at 102$^1/_2$. They are due to mature in 5 years and are currently callable at par.

4. What is the current yield on the Natacomb bonds?
5. What is the rule-of-thumb yield to maturity on these bonds?
6. Will the yield to call be greater than or less than the yield to maturity?

Check your responses by referring to the "Answers to Practical Exercises" section after Chapter 26.

PRICING MUNICIPAL BONDS

There are a great number of municipal bonds outstanding—more than 2 million different issues. They outnumber by a factor of more than 35 the total number of outstanding stocks, options, mutual funds, corporate bonds, and government and agency bonds. Municipal bonds yield less than government bonds not because they are of better quality (they definitely are not) but because of the special tax advantages they may enjoy. The interest on many municipal bonds is tax exempt to holders who purchase bonds issued by their "home" state. This is a tremendous advantage, especially to investors in high tax brackets. Most large issues of municipal bonds and corporate bonds are rated by several agencies; Standard & Poor's and Moody's are probably the best known of these.

Municipal bonds are priced in two ways:

1. As a percentage of their par value, in eighths
2. On a yield-to-maturity basis

Munis (formerly called *tax-exempts*) are usually issued either as term bonds or serial bonds. Term bonds are usually priced according to the first method (as a percentage of par). Serial bonds are usually quoted on a yield-to-maturity basis.

Percentage of Par Pricing

A quick review of Chapter 2 may be in order here, since the method for pricing term municipal bonds is exactly the same as that used for pricing corporate bonds. Term bonds priced in this fashion are sometimes called *dollar bonds*. Prices are expressed in points and eighths such as 98¼, 99⅞, 102, 103½, etc. As with corporate bonds, we can use either of two methods to convert these "quotes" into dollars and cents.

Method 1: First convert any fractional part of the bond's quote into decimal format.

> *Example:* 102$1/2$ becomes 102.5, 97$3/8$ becomes 97.375, etc.

Then multiply by 10.

> *Example:* 102.5 × 10 = $1,025. and 97.375 × 10 = $973.75.

Method 2: First convert any fractional part of the bond's quote into decimal format.

> *Example:* 102$1/2$ becomes 102.5, 97$3/8$ becomes 97.375, etc.

Then move the decimal point one place to the right: 102.5 becomes 1,025. or $1,025; 97.375 becomes 973.75 or $973.75.

Either method gives the dollar value of a single bond (1 M) at the quoted price. For larger blocks of bonds, multiply the single bond dollar value by the number of bonds involved.

These quotes should be thought of as having "percent of par value" written after them!

> *Example:* A bond quoted at 98$3/4$ means that it is trading at 98$3/4$ percent of its par value. A bond quoted at 104$5/8$ is trading at 104$5/8$ percent of its par value.

Learn to think of a term bond's price in terms of its par value. Bonds are traded at par (100), at a discount (less than 100), or at a premium (more than 100).

- Sometimes bonds are trading at a quoted price of exactly 100. We call this price *par*.
- A bond selling at any price below 100 is selling for less than its face value of $1,000 per bond. These are *discount prices*.
- Bonds selling at prices above 100 are trading for more than their face value—more than $1,000 per bond. These are *premium prices*.

> *Example:* The dollar value of 10 bonds (10 M) trading at 102$1/2$ is $10,250. That is, 102.5 × 10 = $1,025. for 1 bond. Multiply by 10 to find the dollar value of 10 bonds.

CALCULATOR GUIDE

▶ 102.5 × 10 × 10 = ◀ **10250.** ($10,250.)

Example: What is the dollar value of 150 bonds (150 M) trading at 97³/₈?

$$97.375 \times 10 = \$973.75$$

This is the dollar value of one bond. Then multiply by the number of bonds (150), for a total of $146,062.50.

$$973.75 \times 150 = \$146,062.50$$

CALCULATOR GUIDE

▶ 97.375 × 10 × 150 = ◀ **146062.5** ($146,062.50)

Yield-to-Maturity Pricing

While term municipal bonds are usually quoted like corporate bonds (as a percentage of par), municipal serial bonds are most often quoted at basis prices, which express their yield to maturity rather than their actual price in dollars. Whereas a term bond quote might read 98¹/₈ or 105³/₄, serial bond quotes might be 4.05 or 5.13.

Example: A quoted offering price of 4.05 means that a bond bought at that price will have a yield to maturity of 4.05 percent. The 5.13 bond is being offered to yield (yield to maturity) 5.13 percent.

Most institutional buyers are not particularly concerned with the specific price they pay for a bond. They feel that it is unimportant whether they pay premium or discount prices. What *is* important to them is the yield they will receive from the investment—what's in it for them! This is best expressed in the bond's yield to maturity, which takes into account the bond's interest payments, length to maturity, and any discount or premium. (Review Chapter 10 for more details on this subject.)

Basis prices are figured using either the yield basis tables or a calculator equipped to figure yields to maturity. The "tombstones" on new issues of serial bonds usually show each bond's "price" as a yield. Traders deal in such bonds on a yield basis.

Example: A quote might read "4.21 bid, offered at 4.19." The bid looks higher than the asked (4.21 versus 4.19), but it actually represents a lower price. The quote is for a bond having a 4.00 percent nominal yield (a 4 percent coupon). Assume that the actual dollar value for a 4.21 bid is $985 (a price of 98½). This is the amount the bidder is willing to pay—$985 a bond—which would give him or her a yield to maturity of 4.21 percent at that price. The seller is asking for more dollars (isn't that what sellers do?) and wants 98⅝ ($986.25) per bond. If the buyer meets this higher price, he or she will only be receiving a yield to maturity of 4.19 percent.

This is logical because the higher the price paid for the bond, the lower the yield to maturity will be. The bond has a fixed interest rate—all buyers receive the same interest—so the lower the price paid for the bond, the higher is the return!

Example: The following quote appears both as a percentage of par and as a yield to maturity:

Bid	Asked	
98½	98⅝	(percentage of par pricing)
4.21	4.19	(yield-to-maturity pricing)

Since both sides of the quote are yields to maturity of more than 4.00 percent, obviously this 4 percent bond is being quoted at discount prices.

- Discount prices always give current yields and yields to maturity that are higher than the bond's nominal yield. The lower price means greater yields.
- Premium prices always give current yields and yields to maturity that are lower than the bond's nominal yield. The higher price means lower yields.

Example: The same bond (4 percent coupon), quoted at premium prices, might look like this:

Bid	Asked	
104¼	104½	(percentage of par pricing)
3.41	3.38	(yield-to-maturity pricing)

SELF-TEST

A. What is the dollar cost for a block of $25,000 par value term municipal bonds trading at 94$\frac{1}{8}$?

B. A municipal serial bond with a 6 percent coupon is quoted "6.01–5.99." Does the bid represent a premium or discount price?

C. A muni quoted "5.54–5.52" has a 5.5 percent coupon. Does the offer represent a premium or discount price?

D. What is the value, in dollars and cents, for a block of 100 (100 M) municipal term bonds trading at 101$\frac{5}{8}$?

ANSWERS TO SELF-TEST

A. $23,531.25. That is, 94.125 × 10 × 25 = $23,531.25.

▶ 94.125 × 10 × 25 = ◀ **23531.25** ($23,531.25)

B. A discount price. Since the bid yield of 6.01 percent is higher than the coupon rate of 6.00 percent, the bond is being bid for at a price less than par. The less-than-par price gives a higher-than-coupon-rate yield.

C. A premium price. The offering yield of 5.52 for a 5.5 percent coupon rate indicates a dollar price of more than par. Premium prices always translate into yields of less than the coupon rate.

D. $101,625. That is, 101.625 × 10 × 100 = $101,625.

▶ 101.625 × 10 × 100 = ◀ **101625.** ($101,625.)

COMPARING TAX-FREE AND TAXABLE YIELDS

Do not neglect to do the "Practical Exercise" at the end of this chapter. It points up the importance of the tax-exempt nature of most muni bond interest payments. Keep in mind that the tax exemption applies only to the *interest* on the bonds, not to any capital gains that may result from trading the bonds. Most investors purchase bonds for their yield—and they are understandably *most* interested in their after-tax yield!

Equivalent Taxable Yield

The interest payments on corporate and Treasury bonds are taxable by the federal government, but the interest on many municipal bonds is exempt from federal taxation. This poses a problem for the investor trying to compare the yields on taxable and tax-exempt securities: How can the yield on a tax-free municipal bond be compared properly with the yield on a taxable investment?

The answer is that investors must compare the dollars they get to keep after taking taxes into consideration. While the dollars of interest earned on a corporate or government bond may be greater than the interest received on a municipal bond, it is necessary to compute how these dollars of interest would compare after accounting for the tax payments due on the corporate/government investments. The total interest payments may be greater on the taxable bonds, but the investor must pay federal tax on these amounts, whereas the municipal bond investor gets to keep the full interest.

The formula used to convert the yield on a tax-exempt municipal issue to the comparable after-tax yield on a taxable issue provides investors with what is known as the *equivalent tax yield*. This calculation permits investors to compare yields on a "fair" basis, taking federal taxes into account. After all, investors should be concerned with the dollars of interest they get to keep after taxes.

$$\text{Equivalent taxable yield} = \frac{\text{tax-exempt yield}}{1 - \text{investor's tax-bracket percent}}$$

Example: For an investor in the 28 percent tax bracket, a tax-exempt yield of 4.25 percent is equivalent to a taxable yield of 5.90 percent:

$$\text{Equivalent taxable yield} = \frac{4.25}{1 - .28} = \frac{4.25}{.72} = 5.90 \; percent$$

Note: In the denominator (the bottom number), you must express the investor's tax bracket in decimal form. Thus a 28 percent tax bracket is entered as 0.28, a 33 percent tax bracket is written as 0.33, etc.

The calculation shows that the investor would receive the same amount of after-tax dollars from a tax-free municipal bond with a yield of 4.25 percent as he or she would from a taxable bond with a yield of 5.90 percent.

CALCULATOR GUIDE

▶ 1 − .28 M+ 4.25 ÷ Mrc = ◀ **5.9027777** (5.90%)

Note: M+ indicates the memory-plus key; Mrc indicates the memory-recall/clear key.

This formula may be used by an investor who is being offered a municipal bond with a yield to maturity of 4.25 percent. If he or she is thinking of switching some of his or her taxable bond holdings into tax-exempt munis, he or she must appreciate that he or she will be losing ground, interest-wise, if he or she sells any of the corporate bonds that yield more than 5.90 percent. If this investor owns 5.90 percent corporates, he or she will earn the same number of dollars after taxes with a muni bond yielding 4.25 percent and more after taxes with a muni bond yielding more than 4.25 percent.

Note: We are not taking into consideration state taxes, which might further widen the gulf between taxable and nontaxable yields.

Finding the Equivalent Tax-Exempt Yield

The formula can be worked backwards. That is, given an investment with a taxable yield, what tax-exempt yield would result in the same number of dollars "in the pocket"? In this case we start with a corporate or government bond yield and ask, "What yield to maturity would we have to earn on a tax-exempt to receive the same after-tax interest?" After all, quality considerations aside, the investor is primarily interested in earning as much after-tax income as possible.

$$\text{Tax-exempt yield} = \text{taxable yield} \times (1. - \text{tax bracket percent})$$

Example: For an investor in the 30 percent tax bracket, a taxable yield of 6.06 percent is equivalent to a tax-exempt yield of 4.24 percent.

$$\text{Tax-exempt yield} = 6.06 \times (1. - .30) = 6.06 \times 0.7 = 4.24 \text{ percent}$$

The investor would receive the same number of after-tax dollars from a tax-exempt bond with a yield of 4.24 percent that he or she would from a taxable bond with a yield of 6.06 percent.

CALCULATOR GUIDE

▶ 6.06 M+ 1 − .30 × Mrc = ◀ **4.242** (4.24 percent)

Note: Under current tax law, there are relatively few different tax brackets. We are going to take a little license with the following "Self-Test" (as we have in the body of the chapter) and ask questions using tax brackets that presently do not exist.

SELF-TEST

A. What is the taxable equivalent yield for a municipal bond yielding 5.90 percent for an investor in the 40 percent tax bracket?

B. What is the tax-exempt equivalent yield for an investor in the 55 percent tax bracket who is considering the purchase of a taxable bond yielding 8.86?

ANSWERS TO SELF-TEST

A. 9.83 percent. That is, $5.90 \div (1. - .40) = 5.90 \div .6 = 9.83$ percent.

▶ $1 - .40$ M+ $5.90 \div$ Mrc = ◀ **9.8333333** (9.83 percent)

B. 3.99 percent. That is, $8.86 \times (1. - .55) = 3.99$ percent.

▶ 8.86 M+ $1 - .55 \times$ Mrc = ◀ **3.987** (3.99 percent)

Note: Notice the dramatic difference. For a person in the 55 percent tax bracket, it would only take a tax-exempt yield of less than 4 percent to equal a taxable yield of 8.86 percent. Such disparities did obtain not too many years ago when the highest tax brackets were high indeed. The higher one's tax bracket, the greater is the tax saving.

PRACTICAL EXERCISE

▶▶ An investor in the 30 percent tax bracket is considering the purchase of general obligation (GO) bonds, at par, issued by the state in which he resides. The GOs have an interest rate of 4.35 percent.

▶▶ He is also considering the purchase, also at par, of the same principal amount of 6.05% corporate bonds issued by the BYO Corporation. BYO is also incorporated in the investor's home state.

1. Which issue, the municipal bond or the corporate bond, will afford the investor the greatest after-tax yield?

2. Which issue would be better suited for inclusion in the investor's IRA account?

Check your responses by referring to the "Answers to Practical Exercises" section after Chapter 26.

Chapter 13

PRICING TREASURY BILLS

Treasury bills (T-bills) are the single biggest element of the *money market* and are a primary instrument of Federal Reserve monetary policy. Although they have low yields —possibly just above the inflation rate—they are so safe and so liquid that they are a very popular instrument for money managers. They are uniquely quoted and traded— and a round lot is $5,000,000!

Discount Yields

T-bills are *discount instruments*. They do not have a coupon rate and, in fact, do not pay any interest until they mature. EE Savings Bonds and zero-coupon bonds work the same way; such instruments are bought at a discount, and the investor ultimately receives his or her interest when the security is redeemed, at par, when it matures. The difference between the discounted purchase price and the par value represents the investor's interest.

T-bills are quoted to represent the discount at which they are trading. They have no coupons (no interest payments until maturity) and no stated rate of interest. They always trade at a discount from par because they can have no reward for holders beyond payment of par value at maturity.

It is true that some debt instruments trade at a premium for one of two reasons: They may be convertible, or they may have a coupon rate that is higher than newly issued instruments of similar length and similar quality. Neither of these conditions apply to T-bills because they are not convertible and do not have any coupon rate. Therefore, like serial municipal bonds, Treasury bills are quoted on a yield basis. T-bills are actually quoted on a discounted-yield basis rather than based on the yield-to-maturity method described in Chapter 9.

Example: A typical T-bill quote might be "3.31–3.29."

Such quotes are "in hundredths, on terms of a rate of discount," or at least that's what it says in the fine print under the "Treasury Bonds, Notes & Bills" heading in the financial press.

Note that the bid yield is higher than the asked yield for the very same reason as with other instruments quoted on a yield basis. (To review this concept, see Chapter 11.)

Converting a T-Bill Quote to a Dollar Price

Here's the formula for converting a T-bill quote into dollars.

Step 1: Discount =

$$\frac{\textit{par value} \times \textit{bid or offer (in decimal form)} \times \textit{days to maturity}}{360}$$

Step 2: Dollar price = par value − discount

Example: What is the dollar price for $100,000 T-bills maturing in 120 days that are offered at 3.89?

$$\text{Step 1: } \frac{\$100,000 \times .0389 \times 120}{360} = \frac{\$466,800}{360}$$

$$= \$1,296.67 \text{ (}\textit{the discount}\text{)}$$

CALCULATOR GUIDE

▶ 100000 × .0389 × 120 ÷ 360 = ◀ **1296.6666**
($1,296.67)

Step 2: $100,000 − $1,296.67 = $98,703.00 (the *dollar price*)

SELF-TEST

A. What is the dollar value of $50,000 par value of T-bills with 108 days to maturity trading at 5.06?

B. What is the amount of the "spread," in dollars, for $1,000,000 of 76-day T-bills quoted 4.97–4.95? You will have to compare the dollar value for both the bid and the offer prices. The difference between the two values is the *spread*.

ANSWERS TO SELF-TEST

A. $49,241.00. That is, discount =

$$\frac{\$50,000 \times .0506 \times 108}{360} = \frac{\$273,240}{360} = \$759$$

Dollar price = $50,000 − $759 = $49,241

▶ 50000 × .0506 × 108 ÷ 360 = ◀ **759.** ($759.)

▶ 50000 − 759 = ◀ **49241.** ($49,241.)

Note: You can do both steps in one shot [and not have to "remember" the answer to the first step (759)] by the following:

▶ 50000 × .0506 × 108 ÷ 360 M+ +/− + 50000 =
◀ **49241.** ($49,241.)

M+ is the memory plus key, +/− is the reverse sign key, and + is the plus key.

B. $42.20. The dollar price of the bid is $989,507.80, and the dollar price of the offer is $989,550.00. The difference between the two figures is only $42.20, typical of the very tight spreads in the T-bill market. The math works out this way:

Discount for the *bid*

$$= \frac{\$1,000,000 \times .0497 \times 76}{360} = \frac{\$3,777,200}{360} = \$10,492.22$$

Dollar value of the *bid*
$$= \$1,000,000 − \$10,492.22 = \$989,507.80$$

Note: The discount and the dollar value will add up to 2 cents more than $1,000,000, as in this instance, if you are using a simple 8-place calculator.

Discount for the *offer*

$$= \frac{\$1,000,000 \times .0495 \times 76}{360} = \frac{\$3,762,200}{360} = \$10,450.00$$

Dollar value of the *offer*
$$= \$1,000,000 − \$10,450 = \$989,550.00$$

The spread is the difference between the two dollar prices, $42.20 ($989,550.00 − $998,507.80), which is typical for the very tight spreads in the T-bill market.

Note: These last questions were tough ones, probably well beyond anything they might test on the series 7 examination. You will certainly be expected to recognize a typical T-bill quote and to appreciate that T-bills:

- Are the shortest-term government instruments
- Have no stated rate of return (no coupons)
- Are not callable
- Are book entry (not issued in physical form)
- Always trade at a discount and are quoted on a discount yield basis

Coupon-Equivalent Yields

The financial press typically prints T-bill information like this:

	TREASURY BILLS				
Maturity	*Days to Maturity*	*Bid*	*Asked*	*Change*	*Asked Yield*
February 21	109	5.85	5.83	+0.01	6.02

The "Asked Yield" column is sometimes referred to as the *coupon-equivalent yield.* Investors realize that T-bills are quoted on a discounted yield basis, which differs from the way yields are expressed for other debt instruments such as corporate bonds and even government bonds. This last column, the "Asked Yield" column, adjusts the T-bill's discounted yield to make it more in line with other bond yields—with other debt instruments that *do* pay coupons regularly. It would be misleading to compare a discounted yield with a "regular" (coupon) yield. The Asked Yield adjustment permits investors to more closely compare apples with apples.

To convert a T-bill's discount yield to a coupon-equivalent yield, apply the following formula:

$$Coupon\text{-}equivalent\ yield\ = \frac{discount}{dollar\ price} \times \frac{365}{days\ to\ maturity}$$

Example: What is the coupon-equivalent yield for $1,000,000 of 109-day T-bills offered at a 5.83 discount yield?

The first step is to work out the discount and the dollar price (as we did in the first part of this chapter):

$$\text{Discount} = \$1,000,000 \times .0583 \times \frac{109}{360} = \$17,651.94$$

$$\text{Dollar price} = \$1,000,000 - \$17,651.94 = \$982,348.10$$

The dollar price is actually very slightly different ($982,348.*06*), but that's because we are using a simple 8-place calculator. Hey, what's the big deal about a four-cent difference when we're dealing with a million dollars' worth of T-bills?

Now we have the numbers to substitute in the coupon-equivalent yield formula:

$$\frac{Discount}{Dollar\ price} \times \frac{365}{days\ to\ maturity}$$

$$= \frac{\$17,651.94}{\$982,348.10} \times \frac{365}{109} = 6.02\ percent$$

Note: The coupon-equivalent yield will always be higher than the discount yield.

There will be no "Self-Test" on this formula because it is well beyond the scope of the series 7 exam.

Chapter 14

MUTUAL FUNDS

This chapter will be much longer—and more detailed—than the other chapters in this book due to the tremendous popularity of mutual funds—and to the level of knowledge demanded of salespeople who offer these widely held investment vehicles to the investing public. Understandably, the regulatory authorities place a great deal of emphasis on this subject when testing salespeople for the series 6 ("Investment Companies, Variable Contracts") or the series 7 ("Registered Representative") examinations.

Mutual funds, also known as *open-end investment companies*, are one of the most popular investment products in the United States. There are thousands of them, and many are used for retirement accounts. Until fairly recently, mutual funds were only traded over the counter, but early in the twenty-first century, a new breed of funds was developed: *exchange-traded funds* (ETFs). ETFs trade differently from the more traditional mutual funds; this chapter will deal only with the older, more traditional funds.

A typical quote for a loaded fund (i.e., a fund with a sales charge) might read "8.80–9.36." This fund has a net asset value of $8.80 and an offer price of $9.36 per share. These are not the typical highest-bid and lowest-offer quotations established in the open market for stocks and bonds. Most of the more widely read financial newspapers, including the *Wall Street Journal* and the *New York Times*, no longer list a two-sided market; they show only the fund's net asset value (NAV) and either net change and/or return figures rather than the fund's offer price.

- *A mutual fund's bid* is, in effect, its liquidating value; it is its *net asset value per share* (NAV), what you would receive if you were to sell (redeem) a share of the fund.
- *The offer* price is the net asset value plus the sales charge, if any, or what it would cost to buy a share of the fund.

A *no-load fund* (i.e., a fund without a sales charge) might be quoted as "12.45–NL." This fund has both a NAV and an offer price of $12.45 per share because there is no sales charge. Some funds also advertise their no-load status by repeating their net asset value for their offer price, such as "13.31–13.31."

To establish the total market value for any mutual fund shares held, simply multiply the number of shares owned by the fund's net asset value:

Total market value = number of shares × net asset value

Example: What is the total market value of a holding of 453 shares of a mutual fund quoted at 21.08–23.04?

Total market value = number of shares × net asset value
                   = 453 × $21.08 = $9,549.24

Note: You multiply by the net asset value because ordinarily that is the price you receive when you redeem mutual fund shares. Certain funds charge a redemption fee or back-end load, and if so, the actual liquidating value will be lower than that arrived at in the formula.

CALCULATOR GUIDE

▶ 453 × 21.08 = ◀ **9549.24** ($9,549.24)

Investors usually add to their original purchases of mutual fund shares by reinvesting the distributions (dividends, interest, and capital gains) of their funds in additional shares—effectively a *dividend reinvestment plan.* Mutual fund shareholders, while building toward a specific investment goal such as retirement, very often reinvest every penny of such distributions, buying additional full and fractional shares. Unlike most common stocks—which only come in full-share lots—mutual fund positions are calculated to three or even four decimal places—this is down to the thousandth or the ten-thousandth of a share!

SELF-TEST

A. An investor has holdings of two mutual funds: 832.479 shares of Marobeth Fund (quoted at 12.33–13.48) and 1,330.638 shares of Bradlini Fund (quoted at 8.86–9.23). What is the total dollar value of his or her fund holdings?

B. What would be the dollar cost of purchasing 739 shares of Euclid Fund quoted at 20.09–21.37?

ANSWERS TO SELF-TEST

A. $22,053.92

Marobeth Fund	832.479 × $12.33 = $10,264.47
Bradlini Fund	1,330.638 × $8.86 = $11,789.45

CALCULATOR GUIDE

▶ 832.479 × 12.33 M+ 1,330.638 × 8.86 M+ Mrc ◀
22053.918 ($22,053.92)

Note: M+ indicates the memory-plus key; Mrc indicates the memory-recall/clear key.

See how using the memory keys made it unnecessary to write down (or remember) the result of the first calculation before doing the second calculation? When you hit M+ the first time, the calculator captures the result of the 832.479 × 12.33 multiplication and puts it in its memory; effectively, it "writes it down on a pad." You then do the second part of the equation (1,330.638 × 8.86), and again, instead of pressing the = key, you hit M+ again, which tells the calculator to add this answer to that same "pad." When you hit Mrc, you are asking the calculator to show you what is now on the pad, which are the two items you entered. It adds them up and shows them to you. Neat, huh?

B. $15,792.43. You simply multiply the number of shares purchased by the offer price, since that price includes the sales charge, that is, 739 × $21.37 = $15,792.43. If 739 shares were being *redeemed*, the "seller" of those shares would receive $14,846.51 (739 × $20.09).

Net Asset Value

A mutual fund's net asset value (NAV) is the actual underlying value of a single share of the fund. In theory, if the entire fund were to be liquidated—if all the assets were sold and all the liabilities were paid off—the NAV per share would be the dollar amount that would be distributed to each share of the fund. Accountants might consider a fund's NAV to be its *book value*.

Each fund figures its NAV (its *bid*) at least once every business day. This requires that the fund first establish a fair market value for every one of its assets—all its stocks, bonds, cash, money-market instruments, and other holdings; all its accumulated interest; all dividends due (past the ex-dividend date but before the payment date); and any other assets. Then the fund must account for all its liabilities. The difference between total assets and total liabilities is the amount of the fund's *net assets*. Dividing this figure by the number of fund shares outstanding gives the net asset value per share (NAV). This computation can be summarized as follows:

$$\text{Net asset value per share } (NAV)$$

$$= \frac{\text{total assets } - \text{ total liabilities}}{\text{number of shares outstanding}}$$

Note: NAV changes as the value of the fund's portfolio goes up and down. Purchases and sales of the fund itself, however, do not usually affect the NAV.

SELF-TEST

A. XYZ Fund has 2,500,000 shares outstanding. It has total assets of $28,000,000 and total liabilities of $5,000,000. What is XYZ Fund's NAV per share?

B. What dollar amount would be received by an investor liquidating 1,750.314 shares of XYZ Fund?

ANSWERS TO SELF-TEST

A. $9.20 ($28,000,000 − $5,000,000 ÷ 2,500,000 = $9.20).

▶ 28000000 − 5000000 ÷ 2500000 = ◀ **9.2** ($9.20)

B. $16,102.89 (1750.314 × $9.20 = $16,102.89).

▶ 1750.314 × 9.20 = ◀ **16102.888** ($16,102.89)

Fund liquidations (redemptions) are effected at the NAV.

Offering Price

An unlisted (non-ETF) mutual fund's offering price can range anywhere from its NAV to approximately 9.3 percent more than the NAV. For example, the "cheapest" price for a mutual fund with a $10.00 NAV would be $10.00 per share. This would represent a no-load fund. It would be quoted either as "10.00–10.00" or "10.00–NL." (The letters *NL* stand for *no load.*)

At the other end of the scale might be a loaded fund whose asked price consists of the NAV plus a sales charge, or *load.*

Example: A mutual fund is quoted as 10.00–10.93. The NAV is $10.00; the asked price is $10.93. The difference between the NAV and the asked price is the sales charge . In this instance, the sales charge (the *load*) is $0.93 (10.93 − 10.00). If you compute this sales charge as a percentage of the bid, it represents a 9.3 percent fee ($0.93 ÷ $10.00 = 9.3 percent). Computed as a percentage of the asked price, the fee works out to 8.5 percent ($0.93 ÷ $10.93 = 8.5 percent).

This is the legal maximum for a noncontractual plan purchase, 8.5 percent, *figured as a percentage of the fund's asked (offering) price.* Many funds are no-load, and most of the load funds levy sales charges much below the legal maximum.

Here's how loaded funds figure their asked (offering) prices:

$$Offer\ price = \frac{NAV}{1 - percent\ sales\ charge}$$

Example: A mutual fund has a NAV of $18.87 and levies a 7 percent sales charge figured as a percentage of the offer price. What is the fund's offer price?

$$Offer\ price = \frac{\$18.87}{1 - .07} = \frac{\$18.87}{0.93} = \$20.29$$

CALCULATOR GUIDE

▶ 1 − .07 M+ 18.87 ÷ Mrc = ◀ **20.290322** ($20.29)

When loaded funds show two-sided quotes (NAV and higher offering price), the offering price shown reflects the *highest* sales charge levied by that fund. Very often the customer is entitled to buy at a sales charge less than the maximum, such as when buying at a *breakpoint* or under *rights of accumulation* (both methods will be described later in this chapter). In such cases, the appropriate offer price must be recalculated.

Example: The fund in the preceding example charges only 5 percent for large purchases. In such cases, the offer price would be $19.86 rather than $20.29. At a 5 percent sales charge (rather than the fund's highest sales charge of 7.0 percent), the calculation would be

$$Offer\ price = \frac{NAV}{1 - percent\ sales\ charge}$$

$$= \frac{\$18.87}{1 - .05} = \frac{\$18.87}{0.95} = \$19.86$$

CALCULATOR GUIDE

▶ 1 − .05 M+ 18.87 ÷ Mrc = ◀ **19.863157** ($19.86)

SELF-TEST

A. Maria Fund has a NAV of $21.24 per share and charges an 8$^{1}/_{2}$ percent sales fee. What is the fund's offering price?

B. The sales charge on the fund described in question A is reduced to 7 percent for purchases between $10,000 and $24,999. What would be the offer price for a $15,000 purchase?

ANSWERS TO SELF-TEST

A. $23.21 [21.24 ÷ (1 − .085) = 21.24 ÷ 0.915 = $23.21].

▶ 1 − .085 M+ 21.24 ÷ Mrc = ◀ **23.213114** ($23.21)

B. $22.84 [21.24 ÷ (1. − .07) = 21.24 ÷ 0.93 = $22.84].

▶ 1 − .07 M+ 21.24 ÷ Mrc = ◀ **22.838709** ($22.84)

Note: The client is not charged 7 percent for the first $10,000 worth of the purchase and 5 percent for the last $5000. The lesser sales charge (5 percent) applies to the entire purchase.

Sales Charges

Sales charges range from zero (no-load funds) to a maximum of 8$^{1}/_{2}$ percent of the offering price (9 percent for contractual plans). Any time a loaded fund's offer price is listed, it always reflects the maximum sales charge. It is possible to calculate a fund's maximum sales charge percentage by dividing its load (the difference between the bid and the asked price) by its asked price:

$$\text{Maximum sales charge} = \frac{\text{offer price} - NAV}{\text{offer price}}$$

Example: A mutual fund is quoted at 14.25–15.49. What is the fund's maximum sales charge, expressed as a percentage of the offering price?

$$\text{Maximum sales charge} = \frac{15.49 - 14.25}{15.49} = 8.0 \ percent$$

CALCULATOR GUIDE

▶ 15.49 − 14.25 ÷ 15.49 × 100 = ◀ **8.00516** (8.0 percent)

Note: The sales charge may be figured as a percentage of the bid or the offer price. Figured as a percentage of the bid, it will be higher than when figured as a percentage of the asked price. A mutual fund's prospectus shows both methods of figuration, but salespersons are permitted to use either method. They usually choose the "percentage of offer price" approach, and this is known as the usual industry method. You also should use this method when taking the series 6 or series 7 examinations.

SELF-TEST

A. What is the percentage sales charge for a mutual fund quoted 9.94–10.69?

B. What is the percentage sales charge for a mutual fund quoted 9.15–10.00?

ANSWERS TO SELF-TEST

A. 7.0 percent (10.69 − 9.94 ÷ 10.69 = 7.0 percent).

▶ 10.69 − 9.94 ÷ 10.69 × 100 = ◀ **7.0159** (7.0 percent)

B. 8.5 percent (10.00 − 9.15 ÷ 10.00 = 8.5 percent).

▶ 10.00 − 9.15 ÷ 10.00 × 100 = ◀ **8.5** (8.5 percent)

Redemption Fees

Some funds charge a redemption fee, which is a fee that is subtracted from the amount received by a person redeeming at NAV. It may be small, such as a fraction of 1 percent, or relatively significant. Redemption fees usually are limited to no-load or low-load funds, whereas other funds may levy a *contingent deferred sales charge*. This is, in effect, a *back-end load*. If a shareholder redeems fund shares relatively soon after having purchased them, the deferred sales charge is high, but it becomes progressively lower over time. There may be no redemption fee at all for shares held for a relatively long time.

Redemption value
= (number of shares × NAV) × (1 − % redemption fee)

Example: What would be the proceeds of the redemption of 1443 shares of a fund with a NAV of $21.47 and a redemption fee of 2 percent?

$$\begin{aligned}
\text{Redemption value} &= \text{(number of shares} \times \text{NAV)} \\
&\quad \times \text{(1} - \text{\% redemption fee)} \\
&= \text{(1,443} \times \text{\$21.47)} \times \text{(1} - .02\text{)} \\
&= 30,981.21 \times 0.98 = \text{\$30,361.59}
\end{aligned}$$

CALCULATOR GUIDE

▶ 1443 × 21.47 M+ 1 − .02 × Mrc = ◀ **30361.585**
($30,361.59)

SELF-TEST

A. What would be the proceeds of the redemption of 1200 shares of a fund with a NAV of $14.88 and a redemption fee of 3/4 of 1 percent?

B. A mutual fund charges a redemption fee of 2.5 percent. It is quoted at $19.66–$20.48. How much money would a client receive after redeeming 12,250 shares?

ANSWERS TO SELF-TEST

A. $17,722.08 [(1,200 × $14.88) × (1 − .0075) = $17,722.08]. (3/4 of 1 percent in decimal format is .0075.)

▶ 1200 × 14.88 M+ 1 − .0075 × Mrc = ◀ **17,722.08**
($17,722.08)

B. $234,814.12 [(12,250 × $19.66 × (1 − .025) = $234,814.12]. Remember to use the bid price when calculating redemption. The offer price is what the fund costs to buy.

▶ 12250 × 19.66 M+ 1 − .025 × Mrc = ◀ **234814.12**
($234,814.12)

Breakpoint Sales

Most loaded funds offer reduced sales charges for bulk purchases. The discounted sales charges vary widely, as do the amounts you have to purchase to receive these reduced charges.

Example: Below is a *breakpoint chart* that is fairly typical for the mutual fund industry. The chart shows that the purchase price will vary with the dollar amount invested. Purchases of the fund in any dollar amount less than $10,000 will incur a sales charge of 8.50 percent. Purchases of $10,000 to $24,999 will be charged only 7.75 percent on the entire purchase. The sales charges are further reduced as detailed in the chart.

Amount of Purchase	Sales Charge (as Percentage of Offer Price)
Less than $10,000	8.50 percent
$10,000 to $24,999	7.75 percent
$25,000 to $49,999	6.00 percent
$50,000 to $99,999	4.50 percent
$100,000 to $249,999	3.50 percent
$250,000 to $399,999	2.50 percent
$400,000 to $599,999	2.00 percent
$600,000 to $4,999,999	1.00 percent
$5,000,000 or more	0.25 percent

Assume that Marobeth Fund has a NAV of $26.82 per share. A $5,000 purchase would be charged 8.50 percent. The offer price for such a purchase would be figured as explained in the "Offering Price" section earlier in this chapter.

$$\text{Offer price} = \frac{\$26.82}{1 - \text{percent sales charge}}$$

$$= \frac{\$28.62}{1 - .085} = \frac{\$28.62}{0.915} = \$31.28$$

CALCULATOR GUIDE

▶ 1 − .085 M+ 28.62 ÷ Mrc = ◀ **31.278688** ($31.28)

Example: Figure the offering price for a $60,000 purchase of the Marobeth Fund in the preceding example.

A $60,000 purchase, according to the chart, would only incur a 4.5 percent sales charge. In decimal form, 4.5 percent is .045.

$$\frac{\$28.62}{1 - .045} = \frac{\$28.62}{0.955} = \$29.97$$

CALCULATOR GUIDE

▶ 1 − .045 M+ 28.62 ÷ Mrc = ◀ **29.968586** ($29.97)

The $5,000 purchase would be effected at an offering price of $31.28 (8.5 percent sales charge), and the investor would receive 159.847 shares:

$$\$5,000 \div 31.28 = 159.847$$

A purchase of $60,000 would be made at an offer price of $29.97 (4.5 percent sales charge), and the investor would receive 2002.002 shares:

$$\$60,000 \div 29.97 = 2,002.002$$

SELF-TEST

Use the breakpoint chart to answer these questions.

A. Given a NAV of $24.50, what would be the offer price used for a purchase of $12,000 worth of Marobeth Fund?
B. How many shares would the customer receive (refer to preceding question)?

ANSWERS TO SELF-TEST

A. $26.56.

$$\frac{\$24.50}{1 - .0775} = \frac{\$24.50}{0.9225} = \$26.56$$

Using the chart, a $12,000 purchase falls within the $10,000 to $24,999 bracket, which calls for a 7.75 percent sales charge.

▶ 1 − .0775 M+ 24.50 ÷ Mrc = ◀ **26.558265** ($26.56)

B. 451.807 shares ($12,000 ÷ $26.56 = 451.807).

▶ 12000 ÷ 26.56 = ◀**451.80722** (451.807 shares)

Right of Accumulation

Many mutual funds permit additional purchases in voluntary (open) accounts at the breakpoint appropriate to the total of the shareholder's previous purchases plus the current purchase. The offer price formula is adjusted to reflect the right of accumulation:

Example: Refer to the breakpoint chart. Kristen Cartlidge has bought shares of Marobeth Fund over the past several years and now owns a total of $49,250 worth of the fund, valued at the current offering price. If she now makes an additional purchase of $5,000, she will only be required to pay a sales charge of 4.50 percent because the value of her "old" shares ($49,250) added to the value of the shares she is now purchasing ($5,000) puts the new purchase in the $50,000 to $99,999 bracket. It is too late to adjust the sales charge on the previous purchases because they were effected over a number of years, but the new purchase qualifies for the reduced sales charge. Assume that the current bid (NAV) is $26.46.

$$\frac{\$26.46}{1 - .045} = \frac{\$26.46}{0.955} = \$27.71$$

Miss Cartlidge will be able to make her new purchase ($5,000 worth) at the offering price that normally would apply to a purchase of $50,000 to $99,999. Note that the reduced sales charge applies to her entire new purchase, not just to the amount in excess of a total holding of $50,000.

CALCULATOR GUIDE

▶ 1 − .045 M+ 26.46 ÷ Mrc = ◀**27.706806** ($27.71)

SELF-TEST

Use the breakpoint chart to answer these questions. Assume a current bid price for the fund of $20.38.

A. James Treanor owns $9,000 worth of Marobeth Fund—figured at the offering price—that he has bought over the past several years. He now wishes to

make an additional investment of $3,000 in the fund.
At what offering price will his new purchase be
effected?

B. How many shares will Mr. Treanor receive from this
new purchase? Figure your answer to three decimal
places.

ANSWERS TO SELF-TEST

A. $22.09.

$$\frac{\$20.38}{1 - .0775} = \frac{\$20.38}{0.9225} = \$22.09$$

He will buy at the 7.75 percent sales charge because
his "old" holdings ($9,000) and his new purchase
($3,000) will put his total holdings in the $10,000 to
$24,999 bracket.

▶ 1 − .0775 M+ 20.38 ÷ Mrc = ◀ **22.09214** ($22.09)

B. 135.808 shares ($3,000 ÷ $22.09 = 135.808).

▶ 3000 ÷ 22.09 = ◀ **135.80805** (135.808 shares)

PRACTICAL EXERCISE

▸▸ Figure all offering prices to the nearest cent.

▸▸ Figure the percentage sales charge to *one* decimal
place.

▸▸ Figure number of shares to *three* decimal places.

1. Geyser Fund has a net asset value of $14.48 and
levies the legal maximum sales charge for a
voluntary plan. What is the fund's offering price?

2. Smallville Fund is quoted 12.48–13.28. What is the
fund's maximum sales charge expressed in the usual
industry manner?

3. Maximillian Fund has a net asset value of $9.88 and
levies a sales charge (expressed as a percentage of the
offering price) of 7 percent for purchases of up to
$10,000, 5 percent for purchases between $10,000
and $25,000, and 3 percent for purchases over
$25,000. How many shares would be purchased by a
client ordering $30,000 worth of the fund?

*Check your responses by referring to the "Answers to Practical
Exercises" section after Chapter 26.*

Chapter 15

RIGHTS OFFERINGS

Not all corporations issue rights—only those which have a preemptive-rights clause in their charter. Rights enable existing common shareholders to maintain their proportionate share of ownership when additional common stock is issued. For example, if Fred Mertz owned 100 of the 1,000,000 common shares outstanding in the Bradlini Corporation, he would own .01 percent of the company. If the corporation then offered an additional 1,000,000 shares of common stock to other investors, Fred's ownership would be reduced to .005 percent. Had the company offered preemptive rights, Fred would have been given the opportunity to purchase 100 of the new shares and thus would have then owned 200 shares, maintaining his ownership at .01 percent.

During a rights offering, the rights to subscribe to the new stock are distributed to the old shareholders, always on a one-right-per-old-share basis. The number of those rights needed to subscribe to a new share, however, is established by the ratio of old shares to new shares:

Rights to subscribe = shares outstanding ÷ new shares

Example: If a company with 1,000,000 old shares outstanding wishes to issue 200,000 shares of new stock, it will require 5 rights to subscribe to 1 new share. If there are 1,000,000 old shares to begin with, and each old share receives 1 right, then 1,000,000 rights will be issued that will be used to subscribe to the 200,000 new shares.

Number of rights needed to subscribe to 1 new share
= shares outstanding ÷ new shares
= 1,000,000 ÷ 200,000
= 5 rights to subscribe to 1 new share

Theoretical Value

There should be some direct relationship between the market price of the rights and their actual value. Rights are a *derivative* in that their market value is tied to the market value of the underlying stock. If the rights are selling at the "correct" price, they are said to be trading at their *theoretical value*. There are two formulas for determining a right's theoretical value:

- One formula is used when the old stock is trading ex (without) rights. During the old stock's ex-rights period, a purchaser will receive only stock.
- Another formula is used when the old stock is trading cum (with) rights. During the cum-rights period, a purchaser receives one right together with each of the old shares purchased.

Old Stock Trading Ex Rights

When the old stock is trading *ex* rights, the following formula is used:

$$\text{Theoretical value of a right} = \frac{\text{market price} - \text{subscription price}}{\text{number of rights needed to subscribe for 1 new share}}$$

Example: What is the theoretical value of a right in an offering under the following circumstances?

- The old stock is trading at $40 per share (ex rights).
- The subscription price at $38.
- It takes 4 rights to subscribe to 1 new share.

$$\text{Theoretical value of a right} = \frac{\$40 - \$38}{4} = \frac{\$2}{4} = \$0.50$$

CALCULATOR GUIDE

▶ 40 − 38 ÷ 4 = ◀ **0.5** ($0.50)

You can check to see if the theoretical value you arrive at is accurate. After you figure the theoretical value of a right, compare the cost of buying the stock outright with the cost of buying rights at their theoretical value and then subscribing to the shares. You should arrive at an identical cost using either method. If the rights are trading at their theoretical value (commission costs not included), you should pay exactly the same for an outright stock purchase as you would for first buying rights and then subscribing.

Example: Let's check our answer in the preceding example by comparing the costs of buying 1 share of old stock versus buying 4 rights and subscribing to 1 share of new stock.

- Buying an old share outright would cost $40.
- Buying the 4 rights necessary to subscribe to a share at their theoretical value of $0.50 each (that's the figure we arrived at in our example) comes to $2 (4 × $0.50).
- Subscribing costs $38.

The total cost of the 1 share of new stock is $40 ($2 + $38), which is the price at which the old stock is trading. The numbers check out!

Old Stock Trading Cum Rights

You must add 1 to the denominator when figuring the value of rights during the period that the old stock is trading cum rights. The formula becomes

$$\text{Theoretical value of a right} = \frac{\text{market price} - \text{subscription price}}{\text{number of rights needed to subscribe to 1 new share} + 1}$$

Example: What is the theoretical value of a right in the following offering?

- The old stock is trading at $58.50 per share (cum rights).
- The subscription price is $56.85.
- It requires 7 rights to subscribe to 1 new share.

$$\text{Theoretical value of a right} = \frac{\$58.50 - \$56.85}{7 + 1} = \frac{\$1.65}{8} = \$0.21$$

CALCULATOR GUIDE

▶ 7 + 1 M+ 58.50 − 56.85 ÷ Mrc = ◀ **0.20625** ($0.21)

Let's again check our answer by comparing the cost of an outright purchase of a share with the buy rights and subscribe cost.

Example: Buying a share of stock outright would cost $58.50, but since the stock is trading cum rights, you also get one right with the stock. You, of course, can sell this right immediately at its theoretical value of $0.21, reducing your overall cost to just $58.29 ($58.50 − $0.21 = $58.29).

If you subscribed to a share by buying the required 7 rights at $0.21 each and paying the subscription price of $56.85, you would be spending the same amount as for the outright purchase of a share (7 × $0.21 + $56.85 = $58.32)!

Note: The 3 cent difference ($58.29 versus $58.32) is accounted for by our rounding off in the first step.

SELF-TEST

A. CYA Corporation has 10,000,000 common shares outstanding and is issuing, through a rights offering, 1,000,000 new shares. The subscription price is $94.00, and the current price of the "old" stock, ex rights, is $93.00. What is the theoretical value of a right?

B. The POS Corporation's "old" stock is currently trading at $77.25, cum rights. The subscription price for the new stock is $75.90, and it requires 8 rights to subscribe to 1 new share. What is the theoretical value of POS rights?

ANSWERS TO SELF-TEST

A. $0.10 [($94.00 − $93.00) ÷ 10 = $0.10].

▶ 94.00 − 93.00 ÷ 10 = ◀ **0.1** ($0.10)

Where did the figure 10 come from? Since there are 10,000,000 shares currently outstanding and only one-tenth of that number of new shares are to be issued, it will require 10 rights to subscribe to 1 new share. You divide the number of old shares by the number of new shares to arrive at the how many rights does it take to subscribe to 1 new share figure, that is, $10,000,000 \div 1,000,000 = 10$.

B. 0.15 $[(\$77.25 - \$75.90) \div (8 + 1) = \$1.35 \div 9 = \$0.15]$.

▶ $8 + 1$ M+ $77.25 - 75.90 \div$ Mrc = ◀ **0.15** ($0.15)

Note: Remember to completely clear the calculator between problems, especially after using the memory function. You must purge the calculator of that letter "M" in the upper left-hand corner of the window. To do this, depress the Mrc key at least twice.

PRACTICAL EXERCISE

▸ The Monaghan Corporation is going to offer 1,000,000 shares of additional common stock through a rights offering. The company presently has 5,000,000 common shares outstanding. The per-share subscription price for the new shares will be $79.00.

▸▸ Ms Tracey Moreno currently owns 150 shares of the "old stock."

1. How many subscription rights will Ms Moreno receive?

2. How many new shares will she be entitled to subscribe to?

3. Presuming that she chooses to subscribe, how much additional money must Ms Moreno invest?

4. If she chooses *not* to subscribe to the new shares but simply to retain the shares she already owns, what is her best course of action?

Check your responses by referring to the "Answers to Practical Exercises" section after Chapter 26.

Chapter 16

CONVERTIBLE SECURITIES

Convertible securities seem to offer the best of both possible worlds: (1) They are usually fixed-income securities, which are senior to common stock, and thus they provide predictable, stable income, and (2) They have an added "kicker" in that they may be converted into common stock and thus afford an investor a chance at dramatic capital gains, a feature usually denied to a fixed-income buyer. If the underlying stock does nothing remarkable pricewise, the investor merely holds the convertible and enjoys the income. When and if the common stock rises in price dramatically, the preferred stock will rise along with it! The preferred stock then becomes a *derivative*.

Why then does anyone ever buy a *nonconvertible* fixed-income security? Why deny yourself the opportunity for a large price increase? There is no free lunch on Wall Street. There *is* a cost for this conversion feature, and this is reflected in the yield on the convertible instrument. A *straight* (nonconvertible) preferred stock—all other things being equal—will yield more than a convertible preferred stock of the same quality. If you want the kicker, be prepared to pay for it by accepting a lower-than-market return on the convertible.

Some preferred stocks and corporate bonds are convertible into other securities, usually the common stock of the company issuing the fixed-income security. Those considering the purchase of a convertible security should know how many shares of common stock they will receive if and when they convert. The literature available to financial professionals describes the convertibility feature as a conversion *price*. Financial professionals translate the conversion price into the conversion *ratio*, which is much more easily understood by the investing public.

Conversion Price

The conversion price of a convertible preferred stock or corporate bond is the price at which the security may be converted into another security. The price might be expressed as "convertible at 50" or "convertible @ $50." Sometimes the word *at* is used, and sometimes the symbol @ is used. The literature sometimes lists the conversion price with a dollar sign ($), and sometimes without one.

> *Example:* The following expressions all mean precisely the same thing:
>
>
>
> convertible at $25   convertible @ $25
> convertible at 25   convertible @ 25
>
>
>
> The $25 figure is the conversion *price*.

The conversion price, which is the figure that practicing financial professionals use, is set by the company issuing the convertible security when it is first brought to market.

Conversion Ratio

In order to be more meaningful to the investing public, the conversion price should be restated as the *conversion ratio*. The conversion ratio is the number of shares of common stock that will be received by an investor in exchange for each share of his or her convertible preferred stock. This is much easier to understand for investors who are contemplating the purchase of a convertible security. They want to know how many shares of common stock they will be entitled to if and when they convert. To compute a convertible instrument's conversion ratio, divide its par value by the conversion price. This gives the actual number of shares of common stock that will be received on conversion.

$$Conversion\ ratio = \frac{par\ value\ of\ the\ convertible\ security}{conversion\ price}$$

Example: What is the conversion ratio for a convertible preferred stock (par value $100) that is convertible at 50?

$$Conversion\ ratio = \frac{\$100}{50} = 2$$

The conversion ratio is 2. An investor who converts will receive 2 shares of common stock in exchange for each share of the convertible preferred.

CALCULATOR GUIDE

▶ 100 ÷ 50 = ◀ **2.** (The conversion ratio is 2.)

Do not assume that all preferred stocks have a par value of $100. While $100 is fairly common, there are many others.

Example: If the preferred stock in the preceding example had a par value of $50, its conversion ratio would have been only 1 (50 ÷ 50).

Note: It is easier when making this calculation with convertible bonds because you are always dealing with a par value of $1,000.

SELF-TEST

A. What is the conversion ratio for a $37.50 par value preferred stock convertible at 20?

B. How many shares of common stock will be received in exchange for a debenture convertible at $48.97?

ANSWERS TO SELF-TEST

A. 1.875 ($37.50 ÷ 20 = 1.875 shares).

▶ 37.50 ÷ 20 = ◀ **1.875** (The conversion ratio is 1.875.)

B. 20.42 ($1,000 ÷ 48.97 = 20.42 shares).

▶ 1000 ÷ 48.97 = ◀ **20.420665** (The conversion ratio is 20.42.)

Note: When figuring the conversion ratio for a convertible bond, always use $1,000 as the par value.

When convertible instruments are first issued, they normally have a relatively "clean" conversion ratio such as 20 or 25, but this ratio will change, as it should, when and if the underlying common stock has a split or a stock dividend. In such cases, the convertible security is *protected against dilution*, and the conversion ratio will change to keep things fair.

Example: XYZ issues a $100 par convertible preferred stock with a conversion price of $50. The conversion ratio would be 2. At the time the preferred stock is issued, the company's common stock might be trading for about 45, so there would be no point in paying $100 for the preferred stock and immediately exchanging it for 2 shares of common stock, each trading at 45. You would be paying $100 and receiving common stock worth only $90 (2 shares at $45). People buy this seemingly "out of the money" instrument in anticipation of the common stock eventually selling above $50. If the common stock rises to 60, then the preferred stock—because it is "worth" 2 shares of common stock —must trade for at least $120. But what if the common stock, now trading at 60, is split 2 for 1? In theory, the common stock will trade at about 30 after the split, and if the conversion price were not adjusted, the preferred stock's price would fall to 60. This would not be fair. To keep things even, the preferred stock's conversion price also would be "split" 2 for 1 and changed to $25. After the adjustment, the new conversion ratio would be 4. Similar adjustments are made for stock dividends paid on the common stock.

Parity

When a convertible security and its underlying common stock are trading at "balanced" prices, they are said to be at *parity*. This means that the package of common stocks receivable on conversion and the convertible security are selling for equal dollar amounts.

Example: A convertible bond is trading at 120 ($1,200) and the underlying common stock is trading at 60. The bond is convertible @ 50.

First, change the conversion price to the conversion ratio (it is a lot easier to work with) by dividing the convertible's par value by the conversion price:

$$Conversion\ ratio = \frac{\$1,000}{50} = 20$$

The bond is trading for $1,200, but its *par* value is $1,000. You have now changed the conversion price of 50 to a conversion ratio of 20. This means that the bond can be converted into 20 shares of common stock. The bond is trading at parity with the common stock if and when its market price and the total market price of the 20 shares of common stock into which it is convertible are the same.

Let's compare the price of the bond and the value of the shares into which it is convertible:

Convertible bond trading at 120 = $1,200
20 shares of common stock trading at 60 = $1,200

The securities are at parity. This is demonstrated by the fact that the market value of the convertible bond ($1,200) and the market value of the 20 shares of common stock into which it is convertible (20 × $60 = $1,200) are the same.

SELF-TEST

A. A convertible bond has a conversion ratio of 25. The common stock into which it is convertible is trading at 43.40. What is parity for the convertible bond?

B. A convertible preferred stock ($50 par) has a conversion price of 20 and is trading at 107.25. The common stock into which it is convertible is trading at 41.50. Is the preferred stock trading at, above, or below parity?

ANSWERS TO SELF-TEST

A. $1,085. (108$\frac{1}{2}$). The question gave you the conversion ratio, which indicates that the bond can be exchanged for (converted into) 25 shares of common stock. A parity price for the bond would be the total value of the 25 shares of stock, or $1,085 (25 × 43.40). If the bond is trading at parity with the common stock, it would be quoted at 108$\frac{1}{2}$, which translates to $1,085.

B. Above parity. The first step is to find parity and then to compare it with the actual trading price of the convertible stock. The conversion ratio must be found by dividing the preferred stock's par value by the conversion price, that is, $50 ÷ 20 = 2.5.

This is the conversion ratio—2.5 shares of common stock will be received for every share of convertible preferred stock exchanged. Therefore, the preferred stock would be considered to be trading at parity if and when its price is equal to the value of 2.5 shares of the common stock it may be exchanged for. A parity price for the preferred stock would be equal to the conversion ratio multiplied by the price of the common stock, that is, $2.5 \times 41.50 = 103.75$.

A price of 103.75 would be *parity* for the preferred stock. The question stated that the preferred stock was trading at 107.25, which is $3^{1}/_{2}$ points *above* parity. This is fairly typical for all "in the money" convertible issues—they usually trade at a slight premium to parity.

Arbitrage

When the prices of a convertible instrument and the underlying common stock are not in balance, a *riskless arbitrage* situation may exist. Such opportunities are fleeting and usually can be exploited only by professionals specializing in such activities (arbitrageurs). The following example is exaggerated but illustrative.

> **Example:** A convertible preferred stock is trading at parity with its underlying common stock. The preferred stock may be exchanged for 2 shares of common stock. It is selling for 57.00, exactly 2 times the price of the common stock, which is trading at 28.50. The preferred stock is at parity.
>
> If a flood of buy orders pushes the price of the common stock up dramatically, say, to 31.00, quick-thinking arbitrageurs would buy all the convertible preferred shares they can at any prices below 62.00. Let's assume that they buy a total of 3,000 shares of the convertible preferred stock at various prices between 57.00 and 62.00, with an average price of 60.00 for the preferred shares purchased. They then issue instructions to convert the preferred stock to common stock and immediately sell 6,000 shares of the common stock at 31.00. Thus, by converting the 3,000 preferred stocks they purchased, they receive the 6,000 shares of common stock to deliver against their sale.

Here's the arithmetic:

- They purchase 3,000 shares of preferred stock at an average price of 60.00 per share for a total purchase price of $180,000 ($3,000 × 60).
- They sell 6,000 shares of common stock at 31.00 per share for a total sale price of $186,000 ($6,000 × 31).
- Buying for $180,000 and simultaneously selling for $186,000 nets a profit of $6,000. This is an *arbitrage*! Now that the arbitrageurs have pushed the price of the convertible up to 62.00 with their buying, the preferred stock is selling at parity with the common stock, and the arbitrage opportunity no longer exists.

Forced Conversion

Most convertible instruments are *callable*. When the issue is called, the holder has been put on notice that he or she has only a short time to "switch" the convertible stock or bond into common stock before the convertible instrument will be retired. He or she can either convert during this time or accept the call and give up his or her convertible security for the call money the company is offering.

When the call goes out, holders must decide whether it is in their best interest to accept the call or to convert. If they do not convert into common stock, they will receive the call price in cash. Sometimes it is better to accept the call; sometimes it is more advantageous to convert to common stock.

Example: Joan Bradley owns XYZ convertible preferred stock, $100 par, and is notified that her stock will soon be called at 102.50. The preferred stock's conversion price is $20, and the company's common stock is trading at 19.50. Should Joan accept the call or convert?

If she converts, she will receive 5 shares of common stock ($100 par value ÷ 20 conversion price) trading at 19.50 per share, which would give her a total value of $97.50 (5 × 19.50). If she does not convert and simply accepts the call for $102.50 in cash, she will be better off than converting to $97.50 worth of common stock. Her best course, obviously, would be to accept the call.

Example: Bill Walker owns a convertible bond, convertible at $50. The underlying common stock is trading at 60.50 when the bond is called at 101½. Should Bill accept the call or convert?

If Bill accepts the call, he will receive $1,015.00 in cash (101½) for his bond. If he converts, he will receive 20 shares of common stock ($1,000 ÷ 50) trading at 60.50 per share, with a total value of $1,210. Bill is better off with $1,210 worth of common stock than with a check for just $1,015. This is an example of a *forced conversion.* It is forced in the sense that Bill must convert in order to receive the higher stock value. Not to convert (to accept the call) would be to lose money.

PRACTICAL EXERCISE

▸▸ An investor is considering the purchase of 100 shares of Mahan Company 8 percent convertible preferred stock, $50 par. The conversion price is 20.00.

1. What is the dollar amount of the total *quarterly* dividend the customer might expect?

2. Should the client purchase the 100 shares of convertible stock and convert at a later date, what will he or she receive in exchange?

3. How might the yield on this preferred stock compare with the yield of another company's "straight" (nonconvertible) preferred of the same quality?

4. What is the preferred issue's relative safety compared with the same company's bonds and common stock?

Check your responses by referring to the "Answers to Practical Exercises" section after Chapter 26.

Chapter 17

BOND AMORTIZATION AND ACCRETION

A poorly understood area, accretion and amortization of bond cost bases, is very often disregarded. Because the concept is a little difficult to understand, that is no excuse for not complying with the tax code. Bond investing—accounted for properly—requires a fair amount of specialized math, some of which we have already explored (yield to maturity, accrued interest). As with all questions pertaining to taxation, please consult a competent professional tax advisor.

Speaking very generally, the cost basis of bonds bought at premium prices must be lowered from time to time; this is called *amortization*. Sometimes the cost of bonds bought at discount prices must be raised from time to time; this is known as *accretion*. Thus a bond's "cost," at least for tax purposes, may change over time because a bondholder's tax-cost basis may change.

The general purpose of such procedures is to properly reflect a fixed-income security's resale or redemption value. This is a rather difficult concept for most investors to grasp—that an investment's cost can change at regular intervals after the purchase has been made.

Amortization

Example: A bond with 10 years remaining to maturity is bought at a price of 109. The bond's purchase price is 109, or $1,090. The premium of $90 over par ($1,090 − $1,000) must be amortized (reduced) each year until maturity. Thus the $90 premium must be scaled down to zero in the tenth year by reducing the cost basis by one-tenth of the premium each year: $90 ÷ 10 years = $9 amortization each year. Thus

- After 1 year, the bond's tax-cost basis has been reduced to $1,081 ($1,090 − $9).
- At the end of the second year, the bond's tax-cost basis is $1,072 [$1,090 − (2 × $9)].
- At the end of the third year, the bond's tax-cost basis would be $1,063 [$1,090 − (3 × 9)], etc.
- By maturity, the bond's tax-cost basis would be $1,000 [$1,090 − (10 × 9)]. Thus there is no loss when a premium bond is held to maturity because, by that time, the bond's cost basis has been reduced to par.

Accretion

Example: An original-issue discount bond with 20 years to maturity is bought in the primary market at 92 ($920). Each year until maturity the bond's cost basis for tax purposes will be increased by annualizing the discount. The discount of $80 (the bond's par value of $1,000 less the purchase price of $920) will be spread out over the years to maturity, and the cost basis will be increased by one-twentieth of the discount ($80 ÷ 20 = $4). Thus

- At the end of the first year, the bond's tax-cost basis will be $924.
- At the end of the second year, the bond's tax-cost basis will be $928.
- At the end of each of the remaining years, the bond's tax-cost basis will be increased by $4—to $932, $936, and so on.
- By the time of maturity, the bond's tax-cost basis has increased all the way to par.

SELF-TEST

A. What is a bond's tax-cost basis after being bought at 124 (when it had 10 years to maturity), held for 5 years, and then sold?

B. A 20-year original-issue discount bond is bought in the primary market at 95 and held for 12 years. It is then sold at 97. What is the profit or loss on this transaction?

ANSWERS TO SELF-TEST

A. 112 ($1,120). The $240 premium (purchase price of $1,240 − the $1,000 to be received at maturity) must be amortized over the bond's 10-year life. The annual amortization is $24 ($240 ÷ 10). After 5 years, the tax-cost basis is $1,120 [$1,240 − (5 × $24)].

B. $10 loss. The tax-cost basis after 12 years will be the original price increased by 12 times the annual accretion. The annual accretion is arrived at by dividing the discount by the years to maturity. The discount is $50 ($1,000 par value − purchase price of $950). The annual accretion is $2.50 ($50 ÷ 20). Thus the tax-cost basis after 12 years is $980 [$950 + (12 × $2.50)]. A sale at 97 ($970) will result in a capital loss of $10 because at the time of the sale the cost basis will be $980.

Chapter 18

BASIC MARGIN TRANSACTIONS

The margin department of a brokerage (now commonly called the *credit department*) has a great deal of responsibility. At least in theory, no security or check may be sent to a client unless the transaction is first cleared by the credit department. The credit department is the firm's last line of defense. Please appreciate that *all* accounts are monitored by the credit department, both cash accounts and margin accounts.

Trading on margin gives investors "leverage." They can buy a greater number of shares dealing on margin rather than for cash. An investor can buy $2 worth of stock for every $1 invested, thus doubling his or her profits if he or she guesses right and the stock goes up. (Do not forget the other side of the coin—if the investor's purchases go down instead of up, he or she will *lose* twice as much.)

The current initial requirement (minimum down payment) for margin purchases is 50 percent, and it has been at this level since 1974. While the Federal Reserve has the right to change the initial requirement, it has not invoked this power for many years and apparently chooses to do other things to affect the economy and trading activity. All our examples in this chapter are based on the current initial requirement of 50 percent.

Market Value, Debit Balance, Equity

Classically, margin accounts are set up like balance sheets. The net worth (equity) in an account is equal to what the securities therein are worth in the marketplace (market value) less whatever the investors owes in the way of margin debt (debit balance):

$$\text{Equity} = \text{market value} - \text{debit balance}$$

The traditional format for a margin account lists the account's market value (assets), its debit balance (liabilities), and its equity (net worth).

Example: A typical margin account might look like this:

Market value	$266,000.	(current value of the securities in the account)
Debit balance	−131,000.	(how much the client owes the brokerage firm)
Equity	$135,000.	

This account contains securities with a current market value of $266,000. (market value). The client owes the brokerage firm carrying the account $131,000. (debit balance). The customer's current "stake" in the account is $135,000. (equity).

The margin account is similar to the situation a homeowner is in some time after having bought a house. Initially, he or she paid part of the purchase price (the down payment) and borrowed the balance from a bank. Some time has passed since he or she bought the new home, and it is now valued at $266,000. The balance of the mortgage is now $131,000.

- The house is now worth $266,000.
- The homeowner still owes the bank $131,000. on the mortgage.
- His or her equity in the house is now $135,000.

Market value	$266,000.	(current value of the home)
Debit balance	−133,000.	(how much the homeowner owes the bank)
Equity	$135,000.	

The homeowner does not have $135,000. in cash, but he or she *would* have that much cash if he or she sold the home for its current market value and paid off the mortgage. Similarly, the equity in your margin account is the amount you would be entitled to receive if the account were liquidated and all loans outstanding against it were paid off.

Initial Requirement

Let's set up an account from scratch.

> ***Example:*** An investor opens a margin account and, as his or her first trade in the account, buys 100 shares of XYZ at 86.00. Here's what the account will look like after the purchase but before the customer has sent any money to the brokerage firm:

Market value	$ 8,600.	(100 shares at 86.00)
Debit balance	− 8,600.	(owed to the broker)
Equity	0	

Since the customer has not yet sent in any money, the entire purchase price was laid out by the brokerage firm. At the moment, the customer is in debt to the brokerage firm for the full amount of the purchase. The customer's equity at this point is zero.

The brokerage firm will send a *margin call* to the customer asking him or her to deposit at least $4,300., which is 50 percent of the purchase price (the initial requirement). The customer must send in at least this amount.

Our investor sends in $4,500., which is a little more than the amount of the call. Here's what the account looks like after the customer's check for $4,500. is deposited into the account:

Market value	$8,600.	(100 shares at 86.00)
Debit balance	− 4,100.	(owed to the broker)
Equity	$4,500.	

The customer's $4,500. deposit reduced his or her debit balance to $4,100. ($8,600. − $4,500.). His or her equity is now $4,500.

SELF-TEST

A. What is the equity in a margin account with a $38,000. market value and a debit balance of $12,500.?

B. The long positions in a margin account are 100 shares of ABC @ 27.50 and 200 shares of DEF @ 67.25. The debit balance in the account is $5,150. What is the customer's equity?

ANSWERS TO SELF-TEST

A. $25,500. Market value ($38,000.) − debit balance ($12,500.) = equity ($25,500.).

B. $11,050. The account's market value is $16,200 (100 ABC @ 27.50 = $2,750. and 200 DEF @ 67.25 = $13,450.).

Market balance	$16,200.
Debit balance	−5,150.
Equity	$11,050.

Margin Calls

Margin calls may be issued when a client establishes a position, either long or short. Margin calls are used to request the required minimum deposit (down payment) on a purchase or a short sale in accordance with the current requirements of the Federal Reserve. A popular misconception is that margin calls are sent out after a market decline. In the strictest sense of the term, *maintenance calls*, not margin calls, are issued when established accounts fall below requirements. More on this later.

The Federal Reserve is concerned only with the required initial deposit. After the appropriate initial deposit is made, the Federal Reserve is effectively out of the picture. As stated previously, the current initial requirement is 50 percent. This means that a client must deposit at least 50 percent of the market value of any securities bought or sold short in a newly opened margin account. An established account may have sufficient "buying power" (explained in Chapter 20) to satisfy the requirement in whole or in part. If such is the case, no margin call may have to be sent to the client.

Example: Mrs. Eileen Meehan, as her first transaction in a margin account, orders the purchase of 1,000 shares of RFQ. The shares are bought at 29.25. What is the amount of the margin call that she will be sent?

The market value of 1,000 shares at 29.25 is $29,250. She will be sent a margin call requesting her to deposit 50 percent of that amount, or $14,625. (0.50 × $29,250). Mrs. Meehan may elect to send in a larger deposit, but her minimum deposit must be at least $14,625.

SELF-TEST

Answer all questions on the assumption that the accounts are newly opened and have no buying power.

A. A client purchases the following in his margin account:

> 100 GHI @ 18.50
> 200 JKL @ 36.00
> 500 MNO @ 88.16

How much money must he deposit?

B. Carol Treanor buys 300 PQR @ 59.00 and sells short 200 STU @ 80.00 in her margin account. What will be the amount of the margin call generated by this activity?

ANSWERS TO SELF-TEST

A. $26,565. The total market value is $53,130.

> 100 GHI @ 18.50 = $1,850.
> 200 JKL @ 36.00 = $7,200.
> 500 MNO @ 88.16 = $44,080.
> $53,130.

Fifty percent of this amount is $26,565. (0.50 × $53,130. = $26,565).

B. $16,850. The total market value of the transactions, both purchases and short sales, are figured in the margin call. Carol bought 300 PQR @ 59.00 ($17,700) and sold short 200 STU @ 80 ($16,000), for a total market value of $33,700 ($17,700 + $16,000). She will be sent a margin call for 50 percent of this total market value, or $16,850 (0.50 × 33,700 = $16,850).

MARGIN: EXCESS EQUITY AND THE SPECIAL MEMORANDUM ACCOUNT (SMA)

We have explored why people deal on margin (leverage) and how much they have to deposit initially (regulation T). Now it is time to find out what happens if the stocks purchased on margin go up in value. The average investor relies heavily on his or her account executive (AE) for guidance in this area, and AEs must give out correct information so as to avoid serious misunderstandings. Margin trading is a two-edged sword. In simple terms, trading on margin permits an investor to buy $2 worth of stock for every $1 deposited. This doubles an investor's profit if the stocks in the account go up but doubles the losses if the stocks in the account go down.

After the margin call generated by a purchase or a short sale has been satisfied, the values of the margin account (market value, debit balance, equity) will change constantly. If the securities purchased rise in price, the client's equity increases.

Example: Mr. Bill Mahan opens a margin account and purchases 1,000 shares of VWX at 60.00. The total value of the purchase is $60,000. Before Mr. Mahan sends any money to the broker, his account will look like this:

Market value	$60,000	(1,000 VWX @ 60.00)
Debit balance	−60,000	(owed to the broker)
Equity	0	

Mr. Mahan will be sent a margin call for 50 percent of the market value of the securities he has purchased, 50 percent of $60,000, or $30,000. After Mr. Mahan has sent in his check for $30,000, his margin account looks like this:

Market value	$60,000	(1,000 VWX @ 60.00)
Debit balance	−30,000	(owed to the broker)
Equity	$30,000	

Note: When something "happens" in a margin account—a purchase, a sale, money coming into the account, money going out of the account, the securities in the account going up, the securities in the account going down, any kind of activity at all —two of the margin account's three values change. This is a good way to see if you have properly recorded any changes: Make sure that two of the account's three values (market value, debit balance, equity) have changed. Not one value and not three values, just two. If you change only one or all three, then you have made a mistake!

Let's see what happens to a margin account when the security (or securities) in the account rise in price.

Example: If the VWX stock in Mr. Mahan's account goes up to 68.00 per share, then the account will be:

Market value	$68,000	(1,000 VWX @ 68.00)
Debit balance	−30,000	(owed to the broker)
Equity	$38,000	

Note: Two values changed. The account's market value went up because of the rise in the price of VWX, and the customer's equity increased. The stock in the account can now be sold for $68,000, and after the broker takes out the $30,000 debit balance owed him, the customer would be entitled to what's left. If the account were to be liquidated, the customer would be sent a check for $38,000.

Excess Equity

The initial requirement for an account with a $68,000. market value is 50 percent of that amount, or $34,000. This would be the required initial equity for someone who purchased this much stock. In other words, the requirement for a margin account is 50 percent of the account's current market value.

Example: Joe Monaghan, a new customer, wants to follow in Mr. Mahan's footsteps and asks his broker to buy him the same securities that are currently in Mr. Mahan's account. Joe will be required to deposit 50 percent of the current value of the account, or $34,000. Let's compare the two accounts, side by side, after Mr. Monaghan has met his margin call by depositing a check for $34,000 into his account.

	Joe Monaghan	Bill Mahan
Market value	$68,000	$68,000
Debit balance	−34,000	−30,000
Equity	$34,000	$38,000

The *required* equity for a *new* account with a $68,000 market value is 50 percent of that amount, or $34,000. We proved that by setting up a new account and figuring how much equity would be required. Comparing the *required* equity in Mr. Monaghan's account with the actual equity in Mr. Mahan's, we see that Mr. Mahan's account is in excellent shape. He (Bill) is *required* to have an equity of $34,000 for his account, which is now worth $68,000, but in actuality has an *actual* equity (thanks to the upward movement in his stock) of $38,000, which is $4,000 greater than the requirement.

This "extra" equity is known officially as *excess equity,* and it is posted to Mr. Mahan's *special memorandum account* (SMA). Mr. Mahan's excess equity is $4,000 because that is the amount by which the equity in his account ($38,000) exceeds the requirement ($34,000) for an account of that market value. Such comparisons are made by the margin department (now usually called the *credit department*) on a daily basis.

Example: A client buys 100 shares of ABC at 90.00 in a newly opened margin account. He or she deposits the necessary margin after receiving the call. Some time later ABC increases in price to 120. What is the excess equity in the account after the price increase?

Here's the account just after the initial deposit (while the stock was selling at 90.00) and then after the price rise to 120.00.

	ABC @ 90.00		ABC @ 120.00	
Market value	$9,000	(100 @ 90)	$12,000	(100 @ 120)
Debit balance	−4,500	(owed the broker)	−4,500	(owed the broker)
Equity	$4,500		$7,500	

The *required equity* for the account, which now has a market value of $12,000, is 50 percent of that amount, or $6,000. The account now has an *actual* equity of $7,500, which is $1,500 in excess of the requirement. That $1,500 excess over requirement is the excess equity, or SMA.

SELF-TEST

A. What is the excess equity in an account with a $110,000 market value and a debit balance of $46,000?

B. A margin account has the following long positions:

100 CDE @ 40
200 FGH @ 70
500 IJK @ 20
1,000 LMN @ 104

and a debit balance of $74,000. What is the account's excess equity, if any?

ANSWERS TO SELF-TEST

A. $9,000.

Market value	$110,000
Debit balance	−46,000
Equity	$ 64,000

The account has an equity of $64,000. The requirement is 50 percent of market value, which is $55,000 (0.50 × $110,000). The actual equity ($64,000) minus the requirement ($55,000) gives excess equity of $9,000.

B. Zero. There is no excess equity in the account because the actual equity does *not* exceed the requirement. The account has a market value of $132,000.

$$
\begin{array}{rcl}
100 \text{ CDE @ } 40 & = & \$4,000. \\
200 \text{ FGH @ } 70 & = & 14,000. \\
500 \text{ IJK @ } 20 & = & 10,000. \\
\underline{1,000 \text{ LMN @ } 104} & = & \underline{104,000.} \\
& & \$132,000.
\end{array}
$$

This market value, less the debit of $74,000, leaves an equity of $58,000. The requirement for an account with a market value of $132,000 is 50 percent of that amount, or $66,000 (0.50 × $132,000). The equity in the account is less than the requirement, so there is no excess equity and no SMA.

Note: An account with no excess equity is known as a restricted account.

Special Memorandum Account (SMA)

When an account's equity exceeds the requirement, excess equity (SMA) is created. A note is made of such excess equity in a "side" account known as the *special memorandum account.* Interestingly, once SMA is credited to the account, it remains there until used; it does not disappear even if the account loses the extra market value that created the SMA in the first place! Stocks going up in price in a long margin account create SMA. Once SMA is credited, a later downside movement in stock prices does not decrease the SMA.

This is why some accounts may be restricted (their equity is less than the requirement) but nevertheless have SMA! The SMA was created earlier in the account's history when the stocks that were bought went above their original purchase prices.

SMA is also created, or increased, when

- A security long in the account is sold. The SMA is automatically credited with one-half the proceeds of any long sale.
- The client sends in cash to reduce the account's debit balance. Any activity that causes the account's equity to increase above its requirement will increase the SMA.

This SMA is a line of credit. It is a notation to the effect that an account has a credit line, which may be used either to buy additional stock or to make cash withdrawals.

While SMA usually can be used for additional stock purchases, there are restrictions on using it to withdraw cash. More on this last point later.

Example: An account with an SMA of $12,000 sells $10,000 worth of stock. What is the new SMA?

Half the proceeds of the sale (0.50 × $10,000 = $5,000) get added to the previous SMA. Thus $12,000 + $5,000 equals the new SMA of $17,000.

SELF-TEST

A. An account sets up this way:

Market value	$120,000	
Debit balance	−65,000	
Equity	$ 55,000	SMA 0

The client wishes to reduce his or her debit balance and sends in a check for $20,000. What is the SMA after the check is credited to the account?

B. A margin account is long 400 CYA @ 64.00 and 1,000 RFQ @ 55.00 and has an SMA of $25,000. If the client sells 100 CYA and 200 RFQ, what will be his or her new SMA?

ANSWERS TO SELF-TEST

A. $15,000. After the client sends in the check for $20,000, the account looks this way:

Market value	$120,000
Debit balance	−45,000
Equity	$ 75,000

Note that the debit balance has been reduced from $65,000 to $45,000 by the cash that was added to the account. The requirement for the account is $60,000 (50 percent of the market value). The equity in the account now exceeds the requirement by $15,000, which becomes the new SMA.

B. $33,700. The SMA will be increased by 50 percent of the proceeds of the sales. Also, 100 CYA @ 64.00 ($6,400) and 200 RFQ @ 55.00 ($11,000) add up to $17,400 worth of stock sold. One-half of this amount ($8,700) is added to the "old" SMA to give a new SMA of $33,700.

Chapter 20

MARGIN: BUYING POWER

In these chapters on margin we have not made any provision for the interest that investors must pay on their debit balances. This, of course, affects investment results. Margin clients must leave their securities with the brokerage firm handling their account because the securities are the collateral for the margin loan. The securities will be in *street name* and thus fully negotiable if the brokerage is forced to sell any of the securities because of a maintenance call.

A margin client may buy additional securities—without putting up any additional money—in an amount equal to double the special memorandum account (SMA). (See Chapter 19 for details on excess equity and SMA.) So long as these additional purchases do not exceed the account's buying power, no margin call will be sent. Thus the formula for figuring buying power is simple, assuming that the current regulation T requirement remains unchanged at 50 percent or double the SMA.

$$\text{Buying power} = 2 \times \text{SMA}$$

Example: An account with an SMA of $2,500 has buying power of $5,000. An account with a $13,000 SMA has buying power of $26,000.

A customer's additional purchases might be less than the buying power available and will reduce the remaining buying power and SMA. Or they may be greater than the available buying power, using it and the SMA entirely and generating a margin call for the amount not covered.

Margin calls are offset, dollar for dollar, by an account's SMA.

Example: An account has an SMA of $3,000 (buying power of $6,000). The investor then buys $1,800 of additional stock. The new purchase ordinarily would generate a margin call for one-half the purchase price, or $900. No margin call will be sent, however, because the SMA will be reduced by the amount of the call; that is, it is reduced by $900 to $2,100. The new SMA is $2,100, and the new buying power is twice that amount, $4,200. The $1,800 purchase reduced the SMA by $900 and the buying power by $1,800.

Full Use of Buying Power

Example: An account has an SMA of $13,500 and buying power of $27,000. The client wishes to use this buying power to the fullest extent and buys $27,000 worth of additional securities. The new purchase uses up all the client's SMA ($13,500) and consequently all the client's buying power as well ($27,000). After the new purchases, the account has no SMA and no buying power.

Partial Use of Buying Power

Example: Paul McQuarrie has an SMA of $12,000 in his account (buying power is therefore $24,000). He then purchases $9,000 worth of additional securities. The new purchases use $4,500 of his SMA and $9,000 of his buying power, reducing the SMA to $7,500 and buying power to $15,000.

Overuse of Buying Power

Example: An account has an SMA of $12,500 and buying power of $25,000. An additional $40,000 worth of stock is then purchased. This purchase normally would generate a margin call in the amount of $20,000. The entire SMA, $12,500, can offset only part of the call, and the brokerage firm sends a margin call for the remainder, $7,500. The account then has no SMA and no buying power.

SELF-TEST

A. What is the buying power in an account with an SMA of $3,650?

B. What will be the buying power in an account with an SMA of $4,000 that then sells $9,000 worth of stock?

C. An account sets up this way: market value $46,000 with a debit balance of $29,000. Does this account have any buying power?

ANSWERS TO SELF-TEST

A. $7,300. The buying power is twice the SMA, that is, $2 \times \$3,650 = \$7,300$.

B. $17,000. The beginning SMA of $4,000 will be increased by half the proceeds of the stock sold. Thus $\$4,000 + (0.5 \times \$9,000) = 4,000 + 4,500 = \$8,500$. If the new SMA is $8,500, then the new buying power is twice that amount, or $17,000.

C. Maybe! The account is restricted in that the equity of $17,000 (market value of $46,000 − debit balance of $29,000) is less than the 50 percent requirement of $23,000 (50 percent of market value). However, perhaps the account had been in much better shape previously and still had SMA (and buying power) left over from the "good old days." Remember that an account does not lose SMA when prices decline.

Cash Available

Generally, the SMA can be withdrawn in cash. The exceptions to this rule will be detailed later in this chapter. When a customer withdraws some or all of the SMA in the account, the debit balance increases, and the equity decreases. The client can elect

- Not to use the SMA at all
- To purchase twice the amount of the SMA without sending in additional funds (buying power)
- To withdraw some or all of the SMA in cash (After all, since the SMA is a line of credit, it is understandable that clients with an SMA can borrow more money.)

Example: Mrs. Joan Bradley has the following margin account:

Market value	$80,000.	
Debit balance	−32,000.	
Equity	48,000.	SMA: $8,000.; buying power: $16,000.

Joan can elect to use her SMA to the fullest in two ways:

- By purchasing as much more stock as possible without having to send in additional funds
- By withdrawing as much cash as possible

Her SMA is $8,000 because her equity exceeds the requirement by that amount [equity $48,000, requirement $40,000 (50 percent of market value)]. If Joan decides to use her buying power to the fullest, she may purchase $16,000 of additional securities, raising both her market value and her debit balance by that amount. Her account will then show:

Market value	$96,000.
Debit balance	−48,000.
Equity	$ 48,000. SMA: 0;
	buying power: 0.

She will have used up her entire buying power and will now have no SMA. Notice that her equity is now 50 percent of her market value, exactly in line with the requirement.

If instead of purchasing more stock, Joan decides to withdraw as much cash as possible, she will ask that her full SMA ($8,000) be sent to her. This will increase her debit balance and reduce her equity. Her account will then show:

Market value	$80,000.
Debit balance	−40,000.
Equity	$40,000. SMA: 0;
	buying power: 0.

Again, she will have used up her entire SMA and will now have no buying power. Notice that after this full utilization of SMA, just as after the full utilization of her buying power, the equity in her account is now 50 percent of her market value, exactly in line with the requirement.

Compare the original account with the account as it would appear if it used all the buying power (first example) and then with the account as it would appear if it used all the SMA by withdrawing cash (second example). Note that in each case, two (not one, not three) of the three values changed. In the first instance, the account's market value and debit balance changed; in the second example, the account's debit balance and equity changed.

Exceptions to Cash Withdrawal

There are two important exceptions to the general rule that a margin customer may withdraw the SMA in cash:

- A cash withdrawal may not reduce an account's equity below $2,000.
- A cash withdrawal cannot reduce an account's equity below 25 percent of market value.

Example: A cash withdrawal may not reduce an account's equity below $2,000. An account appears as follows:

Market value	$5,000.	
Debit balance	−2,400.	
Equity	$2,600.	SMA: $1,000;
		buying power: $2,000.

If this client wishes to withdraw as much cash as possible, he or she can only be given $600! To give the client more money would cause the account's equity to fall below $2,000. Let's look at the account after the client has been sent the maximum amount of cash, $600.

Market value	$5,000.	
Debit balance	−3,000.	
Equity	$2,000.	SMA: $400;
		buying power: $800.

Note: The withdrawal of $600 in cash has increased the debit balance and reduced the equity. The SMA is now $400 (and the buying power $800), but the customer cannot withdraw any more cash. To do so would cause the equity in the account to fall below $2,000. The account now serves as an example of one in which there is an SMA and buying power but with no cash available. No cash withdrawals may be made if they reduce equity below 25 percent of market value.

Example: A cash withdrawal cannot reduce an account's equity below 25 percent of market value. An account appears as follows:

Market value	$80,000.
Debit balance	−55,000.
Equity	$25,000. SMA: $9,000;
	buying power: $18,000.

If this client wishes to withdraw as much cash as possible, he or she can only be given $5,000, not the full SMA of $9,000. To give the client more than $5,000 would cause the equity in the account to fall below 25 percent of its market value. Let's look at the account after the client has been sent the maximum amount of cash, $5,000.

Market value	$80,000.
Debit balance	−60,000.
Equity	$20,000. SMA: $4,000;
	buying power: $8,000.

Note: The withdrawal of $5,000 in cash has increased the debit balance and reduced the equity. The SMA is now $4,000 (and the buying power $8,000), but the customer cannot withdraw any more cash because to do so would cause the equity in the account to fall below 25 percent of market value. The account's equity is now exactly 25 percent of its market value. The account still has an SMA, but no cash withdrawals may be made.

In summary, the SMA may be withdrawn in cash unless it would cause the equity to fall below $2,000 or below 25 percent of market value.

SELF-TEST

How much cash may be withdrawn from the following accounts?

A. | Market value | $56,000. |
|---|---|
| Debit balance | −27,000. |
| Equity | $29,000. SMA: $10,000; |
| | buying power: $20,000. |

B. | Market value | $56,000. |
|---|---|
| Debit balance | −40,000. |
| Equity | $16,000. SMA: $6,000; |
| | buying power: $12,000. |

C. | Market value | $5,600. |
|---|---|
| Debit balance | −3,500. |
| Equity | $2,100. SMA: $1,400; |
| | buying power: $2,800. |

ANSWERS TO SELF-TEST

A. $10,000. The entire SMA may be withdrawn because doing so would not cause the account to go below $2,000 in equity or for the equity to become less than 25 percent of market value.

Check the answer. Here's the account after the $10,000 withdrawal:

Market value	$56,000.	
Debit balance	−37,000.	
Equity	$19,000.	SMA: 0; buying power: 0.

The equity did not go below $2,000, and the equity is still above 25 percent of the market value.

B. $2,000. The customer may only withdraw $2,000 because this will reduce the equity to $14,000, where it will then be 25 percent of market value. Here's the account after the $2,000 withdrawal:

Market value	$56,000.	
Debit balance	−42,000.	
Equity	$14,000.	SMA: $4,000; buying power: $8,000.

The equity in the account is now 25 percent of the market value, the lowest permissible level.

C. $100. Only $100 may be sent because this will reduce the equity to the lowest permissible minimum of $2,000. Here's the account after the $100 withdrawal:

Market value	$5,600.	
Debit balance	−3,600.	
Equity	$2,000.	SMA: $1,300; buying power: $2,600.

Chapter 21

MARGIN: MAINTENANCE REQUIREMENTS FOR LONG ACCOUNTS

Establishing a position—buying or selling short—will generate a *margin call* if there is insufficient buying power in a margin account. Once the initial requirement (regulation T) is met, the Federal reserve is effectively out of the picture. Should the market run adversely (down for a long account or up for a short account) and the account's equity fall below maintenance requirements, a *maintenance call* will be sent out. The financial press refers to both margin and maintenance calls as *margin calls*. In this book we will distinguish between the two.

Initial Requirement

The initial margin requirement (regulation T), as set by the Federal Reserve, is used to determine

- The minimum deposit that a margin customer must make when creating a position, long or short.
- The margin requirement for an account when determining whether there is any SMA. This margin requirement, currently 50 percent, only comes into play when a security is bought or sold short. After the securities are purchased and margined properly, the Federal Reserve is no longer concerned.

However, other regulatory agencies are concerned. These other institutions include the stock exchanges, the National Association of Securities Dealers (NASD), and brokerage firms. The rules established by these institutions are designed to ensure that customers do not borrow for the purpose of buying securities and then default on their loans. Defaults not only can endanger the brokerage firm carrying the defaulted account(s), but also, if unchecked, can create a destructive domino effect throughout the financial community.

Many individual brokerage firms have their own requirements, which generally are more stringent than those of the New York Stock Exchange (NYSE) and NASD. These firms' *house rules* can be stiffer than those of the regulatory agencies, but they cannot be more lenient. The reason for such rigorous house rules is clear. Since the securities in a brokerage account are the collateral for the debit balance, the lending brokerage firm understandably would be concerned were the market value of the securities long in a margin account worth less than the debit balance. The broker's loan would be in jeopardy if the securities had to be liquidated, since their sale would not generate sufficient cash to pay off the debit balance.

Essentially, this is the reason for all the rules on maintenance. They ensure that accounts in danger of becoming undersecured or completely unsecured are strengthened—or liquidated—before they become big problems.

There are different maintenance requirements for long and short accounts. Long maintenance requirements are described in this chapter; short maintenance requirements will be described in Chapter 22.

Long Maintenance Requirements

A long margin account must maintain an equity of at least 25 percent of the account's market value. This is the long maintenance requirement. The requirement is geared to the market value and has nothing to do with any other element of the account, such as debit balance, special memorandum account (SMA), or buying power. So long as the equity is 25 percent or more of the long market value, the account is properly maintained.

Note: The initial requirement is 50 percent, but thereafter, the maintenance requirement is 25 percent.

Example: What is the maintenance requirement for the following account?

Market value	$120,000.	
Debit balance	−50,000.	
Equity	$70,000.	SMA: $10,000; buying power: $20,000.

The maintenance requirement for the account is $30,000. That is, the equity in the account must be at least 25 percent of the account's long market value. The market value is $120,000, so the maintenance requirement is 25 percent of that, or $30,000 (0.25 × $120,000 = $30,000.).

Note: Brokerage firms may invoke stricter house requirements, such as 30 or 35 percent, and most brokerages do have such rules.

What happens when an account falls below the 25 percent maintenance requirement? A maintenance call is issued, and the client must then bring the account back up to proper levels in one of three different ways:

1. Depositing cash
2. Depositing additional marginable securities
3. Selling securities in the account

Each of these activities calls for different amounts. The amount of cash deposit necessary to satisfy the call, for instance, is not the same as the value of additional securities to be deposited, and a "sellout" is for a still different amount.

Example: The following account will be sent a maintenance call:

Market value	$40,000.	
Debit balance	−33,000.	
Equity	$7,000.	SMA: $1,500; buying power: $3,000.

The maintenance requirement is $10,000, which is 25 percent of the account's long market value (0.25 × $40,000 = $10,000). The account has only $7,000 in equity, which is $3,000 less than the $10,000 requirement. This puts the account on maintenance call for $3,000. The account has an SMA and buying power, but no cash withdrawals would be permitted.

The maintenance call for $3,000 can be met by

1. Depositing cash in the same amount as the call: $3,000 in cash.
2. Depositing additional marginable securities worth one-third more than the margin call: $4/3 \times$ the call of $3,000 = $4,000 in additional securities.
3. Selling securities in the account with a market value of four times the amount of the call: $12,000 would have to be sold.

After the call is met, the account will be structured in three different ways depending on which of the three methods the customer chose to meet the maintenance call:

	Deposit of Cash ($3,000)	Deposit of Marginable Securities Worth $4/3$ the Amount of the Call ($4/3 \times$ $3,000 = $4,000)	Sellout of Securities Worth 4 × the Amount of the Call (4 × $3,000 = $12,000)
Market value	$40,000	$44,000	$28,000
Debit balance	−30,000	−33,000	−21,000
Equity	$10,000	$11,000	$7,000

Depositing cash in the amount of the maintenance call reduced the debit balance by $3,000 and increased the equity by $3,000. The equity is now exactly 25 percent of the market value ($0.25 \times $40,000 = $10,000$), and the account is no longer on maintenance call.

Depositing additional marginable securities into the account, which were worth $4/3$ the amount of the maintenance call, raised the market value and equity by $4,000 each. The equity is now exactly 25 percent of the market value ($0.25 \times $44,000 = $11,000$), and the account is no longer on maintenance call.

Selling $12,000 worth of the securities in the account reduced the market value and the debit balance by $12,000 each. The equity is now exactly 25 percent of the market value ($0.25 \times $28,000 = $7,000$), and the account is no longer on maintenance call.

Note that this client had three different choices to meet the call: $3,000 in cash, $4,000 in additional securities, or a $12,000 sellout.

SELF-TEST

Use the following account to answer the questions.

Market value	$80,000
Debit balance	−60,600
Equity	$19,400

A. What is the amount of the maintenance call on this account?

B. How much cash must be deposited to meet the call?

C. If the call were to be met by depositing additional marginable securities, what value of such securities must be deposited?

D. If the call were to be satisfied by selling some securities in the account, what value of such securities must be sold?

ANSWERS TO SELF-TEST

A. $600. The minimum maintenance requirement is 25 percent of the market value or $20,000 (0.25 × $80,000 = $20,000). The actual equity is just $19,400, which is $600 short of the required amount. This is the amount of the maintenance call.

B. $600. A maintenance call for $600 can be met by depositing that same amount in cash.

C. $800. Meeting a maintenance call by depositing additional marginable securities takes $4/3$ ($1^1/3$) of the amount of the call in stock, that is, $4/3$ × $600 = $800. This is the amount of "new" stock that would have to be deposited to meet the $600 call.

▶ 4 × 600 ÷ 3 = ◀ **800.** ($800.)

D. $2,400. Meeting a call by selling out securities in the account requires that positions valued at four times the amount of the call be sold (4 × $600 = $2,400)

Maintenance Excess

An account's maintenance excess is the amount by which the actual equity exceeds the maintenance requirement. As you have seen, when the account is *below* the maintenance requirement, the brokerage firm sends a maintenance call.

The calculation for maintenance excess is quite simple: You compare the equity with the maintenance requirement.

Example: A long margin account sets up as follows:

Long market value	$50,000
Debit balance	−18,000
Equity	$32,000

- The maintenance requirement is 25 percent of the long market value, or $12,500 (0.25 × $50,000).
- The actual equity is $32,000, which is $19,500 greater than the requirement ($32,000 − $12,500 = $19,500).
- The *maintenance excess* in this account is $19,500.

PRACTICAL EXERCISE

▸ An investor purchases 800 shares of CYA at 75.00 in a newly opened margin account.

1. What will be the structure of the account (market value, debit balance, equity) after the investor meets the regulation T call?

2. What will be the structure of the account if CYA then goes to 90.00?

3. After the move to 90.00, what will be the account's SMA?

4. After the move to 90.00, what will be the account's buying power?

5. After the move to 90, to what amount might the account's market value decline before incurring a maintenance call?

Check your responses by referring to the "Answers to Practical Exercises" section after Chapter 26.

Chapter 22

MARGIN: MAINTENANCE REQUIREMENTS FOR SHORT ACCOUNTS

Go slowly on this chapter. Short accounts are a little more difficult to grasp than long accounts, and things happen more quickly in such an account. When the short securities go down in value (that's what the short seller is looking for), the special memorandum account (SMA) and short selling power build up more quickly than they would for the same percentage favorable move in a long account, but when the short stocks go up in value, they precipitate maintenance calls more quickly than similar moves in long accounts.

When a client sells stock he or she does not own, the transaction is called a *short sale*. To make good the delivery, the brokerage firm borrows shares from someone else. Thus, after the short sale is executed, the client owes the brokerage firm the value of the borrowed stock. Also, since a sale was effected in the account, there is a credit balance for the amount of the short sale.

It is exactly the opposite of a long account. In a long account,

- You own the stock you bought and owe the debit balance created by the purchase.
- The long stock position is positive (+), and the debit balance is negative (−).

In a short account,

- You owe the stock you sold short and own the credit balance created by the short sale.
- The short stock position is negative (−), and the credit balance is positive (+).

The formula for figuring the equity in a *long* account is to subtract the debit balance from the market value:

Equity in long margin account
= long market value − debit balance

The formula for figuring the equity in a short margin account is to subtract the short market value from the credit balance.

Equity in short margin account
= credit balance − short market value

Example: The client sells 1,000 shares of PCI which he or she does not own (a short sale), and the brokerage firm borrows shares from another client's account to make good the delivery. After the order is executed at 80.00 per share but before the client sends in any funds, here's what the account looks like:

Credit balance	$80,000	(the proceeds of the short sale)
Short market value	−80,000	(the value of the borrowed stock owed)
Equity	0	

The account starts out with a credit balance from the short sale. This money came for the sale. The customer did not make delivery of any stock, so the broker borrowed the stock from another source. It is this stock that the customer ultimately must repay.

Initial Requirement

The initial requirement for a short sale is the same as for a long purchase, 50 percent of the market value.

Example: The $80,000 short sale in the preceding example generates a $40,000 margin call (0.50 × $80,000). After the client meets the $40,000 call by sending in a check for that amount, the account sets up this way:

Credit balance	$120,000	(the proceeds of the short sale + the margin deposit)
Short market value	−80,000	(the value of the borrowed stock owed)
Equity	$ 40,000	

The credit balance now totals $120,000; $80,000 came for the sale of the stock, and $40,000 cash was sent in to meet the margin call. Now the equity ($40,000) is 50 percent of the short market value ($80,000).

The initial requirement is the same for long and short margin accounts: The beginning equity must equal at least 50 percent of the market value.

Short Selling Power and SMA

Short accounts that "work" (that is, the short positions go *down* in price) create SMA and short selling power more quickly than do long accounts when the stocks therein go up. On the other hand, when the stocks in a short account rise in price (not a good thing for a short seller), maintenance calls can go out more quickly than when stocks go down in a long account.

Example: Here's what the short account in the preceding example looks like if the price of the short position goes down to 70.00:

Credit balance	$120,000	
Short market value	−70,000	(the *current* value of borrowed stock)
Equity	$50,000	

The requirement for an account with a $70,000 market value is 50 percent of that amount. The account now has a short market value of $70,000, and 50 percent of that amount is $35,000. Comparing the margin *requirement* of $35,000 with the actual equity of $50,000 shows that we have an excess equity of $15,000 ($50,000 − $35,000). This is the account's SMA, $15,000. Doubling the SMA of $15,000 gives short selling power of $30,000.

Maintenance Requirements

The maintenance requirements for short positions are much more stringent than for long positions. You will recall that the long maintenance requirement was an equity of 25 percent of market value. For short positions, the requirements depend on the market price of the short positions. Here is the scale of requirements:

Market Price of Short Position	Maintenance Requirement
0 to 2.50	$2.50 per share
2.50 to 5.00	100 percent
5.00 to 16.66	$5.00 per share
16.67 and higher	30 percent

Example: What is the maintenance requirement for a margin account with the following short positions?

1,000 ABC @ 2
1,000 DEF @ 4
1,000 GHI @ 6
1,000 JKL @ 20

- The maintenance requirement for ABC (in the 0 to 2.50 range) is $2,500 (1,000 shares × $2.50 per share).
- The maintenance requirement for DEF (in the 2.50 to 5.00 range) is $4,000 (100 percent of the value of the position; 1,000 shares @ 4.00 per share = $4,000).
- The maintenance requirement for GHI (in the 5 to 16.66 range) is $5,000 (1,000 shares × $5. per share).
- The maintenance requirement for JKL (in the 16.67 and higher range) is $6,000 (1,000 shares × $20.00 per share × 30 percent).

Adding these four different requirements together gives a *total* maintenance requirement of $17,500 for the account ($2,500 + $4,000 + $5,000 + $6,000).

Note: The lower the price of the stock sold short, the higher is the requirement. This makes sense. When you short a low-priced stock, there is very little that you can make (after all, a stock can only go down to zero), but you can lose a dramatic amount if the stock goes up (theoretically, there is no limit as to how high a stock can go). In effect, when you short a low-priced stock, you have very little to gain but have exposure to a very large loss. The large maintenance requirements on low-priced short positions are meant to discourage speculators from establishing positions where they have very little to gain but are at great risk of large losses.

SELF-TEST

What is the maintenance requirement for the following short account?

Short positions:

100 shares of D @ 50.00

200 shares of E @ 14.50

100 shares of F @ 3.85

1,000 shares of G @ 1.50

ANSWER TO SELF-TEST

$5,385. Each of the short positions has a different maintenance requirement. For 100 D @ 50, the maintenance requirement is $1,500 (30 percent of the market value of the position). For 200 E @ 14.50, the maintenance requirement is $1,000 ($5. per share). For 100 F @ 3.85, the maintenance requirement is $385 (100 percent of the market value of the position). For 1,000 G @ 1.50, the maintenance requirement is $2,500 ($2.50 per share). These individual maintenance requirements *total* $5,385. The short positions have a total short market value of $9,785.

Maintenance Excess

An account's maintenance excess is the amount by which the actual equity exceeds the maintenance requirement. The calculation for maintenance excess is quite simple: You compare the equity to the maintenance requirement.

Using the account in the previous "Self-Test" as an example,

Credit balance	$18,670
Short market value	−$9,785
Equity	$8,885

- We calculated, in the "Self-Test," that the *maintenance requirement* for this account was $5,385.
- The actual equity is $8,885, which is $3,500 greater than the requirement ($8,885 − $5,385 = $3,500).
- The *maintenance excess* in this account is $3,500.

Chapter 23

PRICING OPTIONS

A call option confers on its owner the right to buy; the seller (writer) of the call has the obligation to sell, if asked (exercised). In theory, there is no limit to the profit potential for a long call because there is, in theory, no limit to how high a stock can rise in price. A put option gives its owner the right to sell; the writer of the put has an obligation to buy, if asked (exercised). Options are a *zero-sum game:* Whatever the option buyer makes, the option writer loses, and whatever the option buyer loses, the option writer makes. They both have the same breakeven point. Options are d*erivative* instruments; their prices are influenced directly by the prices of the underlying securities.

Equity Options

Equity (stock) options are priced, like stocks, in dollars and cents. While most stocks have a minimum price variation of only 1 cent ($0.01), many options have minimum price variations of either 5 cents ($0.05) or 10 cents ($0.10).

Each equity option covers 100 shares of the underlying stock. The price quoted in the newspaper (known as the *premium*) must be multiplied by 100 to arrive at the actual dollar cost of the equity option.

Examples:
- A put or call selling for 1.50 costs $150 (1.50 × 100).
- An option priced at 4.75 sells for $475 (4.75 × 100).
- An option trading at 12.45 sells for $1,245 (12.45 × 100).

Aggregate Exercise Price

A call option's aggregate exercise price is the amount of cash that must be put up if and when the option is exercised. This is the actual cost for exercising the option (excluding commission). Again, as we did when figuring the cost of the option itself, we must multiply the strike price by 100 to arrive at the aggregate exercise price.

Example: The aggregate exercise price for a call with a strike price of 35.00 would be $3,500 (35.00 × 100).

SELF-TEST

A. What is the total dollar cost, excluding commissions, to purchase 5 ABC April 40 calls trading at 3.50 and 10 DEF August 70 puts trading at 9.10?

B. What would be the aggregate exercise price for exercising the 5 ABC calls?

ANSWERS TO SELF-TEST

A. $10,850. The ABC calls have a premium (market price) of 3.50, which translates to $350 per call. Five such calls would cost $1,750. The DEF puts are trading at 9.10, which means $910 per option. Ten such options would cost $9,100. The total cost for both the calls and the puts would be $10,850.

▶ 3.50 × 100 × 5 M+ 9.10 × 100 × 10 M+ Mrc = ◀ **10850.** ($10,850.)

B. $20,000. The aggregate exercise price is the amount of money, excluding commissions, that the call owner has to pay to exercise the option. The calls have a strike price (exercise price) of 40, which means that the exerciser has to pay 100 times that amount to exercise one call, or $4,000. He or she has five such calls, so the total cost for exercising all five would be $20,000. Note that the aggregate exercise price does not factor in the original cost of the option.

Note: Stock options can only be purchased for cash. They must be paid for in full. Unhedged options can only be sold (written) in margin accounts.

Foreign Currency Options

The three most actively traded foreign currency options are the British pound, the Euro (ECU), and the Swiss franc. Other foreign currency options include Australian dollars, Canadian dollars, and Japanese yen. To convert *strike prices* to dollars and cents (except for Japanese yen), divide the strike price by 100. *Premiums* are expressed in pennies! A premium of 2.25 is $0.0225; a premium of .8 is $0.008.

In contrast to equity options, which have a unit of trading of 100 shares, trading units for the actively traded currency options vary from 31,250 (British pounds) to 62,500 (Euros and Swiss francs). It is not necessary to memorize these (and the many other) trading units; they are shown in the daily price listings.

The market prices for the various currencies—the *underlying*—are equivalent to the "closing prices" of the underlying stocks for equity options. Again, these prices are in cents per unit for British pounds, Canadian dollars, and Swiss francs and in hundredths of cents per unit for Japanese yen.

To calculate the cost of purchasing a currency option, multiply the unit of trading by the premium. Remember that the premiums are in cents or hundredths of cents per unit.

Example: February British pound calls with a strike price of 145 were trading at 1.55 when the pound's "last" was 147.69 The option gives the owner the right to buy 31,250 British pounds at US$1.45 per pound. The option is "in the money" because the strike is lower than the current market. The premium, in dollars, would be $485.94 ($0.0155 × 31,250).

SELF-TEST

What is the cost of one Swiss franc call with a premium of .75?

ANSWER TO SELF-TEST

$468.75. The unit of trading for Swiss francs is 62,500. A premium of .75 equals $0.0075 (³/4 of 1 cent). Thus

$$62,500 \times \$0.0075 = \$468.75$$

Index Options

In early 2003, the most actively traded index option was the S&P 500 Index (SPX). The trading volume in this option alone exceeded the volume for all the other index options combined.

Index options, like equity options, are traded in dollars and cents. The most common multiplier for index options is 100, just as it is for equity options. Therefore, to arrive at the dollar price of an index option, simply multiply the quoted price (the premium) by 100.

The dollar cost of an S&P 500 call trading at 8.25 would be $825 (100 × $825).

PRACTICAL EXERCISE

▶▶ An ABC September 65.00 call has a premium of 7.50, whereas the underlying stock is trading at 66.25.

1. Is the option in the money, out of the money, or at the money?

2. What is the option's intrinsic value, if any?

3. What is the option's time value, if any?

4. What is the maximum profit potential for a *buyer* of this option?

5. What is the maximum loss potential for a *buyer* of this option?

6. What is the maximum profit potential for the *writer* of this option?

7. What is the maximum loss potential for a naked *writer* of this option?

8. Excluding commissions, what would be the total dollar cost for 10 of these options?

Check your responses by referring to the "Answers to Practical Exercises" section after Chapter 26.

Chapter 24

OPTIONS MARGIN

Options can only be *purchased* for cash—and can only be *sold* (written) in margin accounts. Since some margin requirements are reduced for out-of-the-money options, let's review the concepts of in, at, and out of the money. In general, options are in the money when it is profitable to exercise them, and out of the money when it is not profitable to exercise them. For this purpose, you do *not* consider the option's premium, just whether the strike price is more favorable—or less favorable—than the market price of the underlying stock. In-the-money options have intrinsic value, whereas at-the-money and out-of-the-money options have no intrinsic value.

Calls

A call option is

- In the money when it is profitable to exercise the option and to immediately resell the underlying in the secondary market. This condition obtains when the call's strike price is less than the current market price of the underlying.

- Out of the money when its strike price is higher than the underlying's market price. Someone exercising the call and immediately reselling the underlying in the secondary market would suffer a loss.

- At the money when the underlying is selling at the strike price. Someone who exercises the call and immediately resells the underlying in the secondary market would have neither a profit nor a loss.

Examples:
- An XYZ 50 call is in the money when XYZ is selling in the open market for any price higher than 50. If XYZ is trading at 53.50, then the 50 call option is *in*

the money by 3.50 points. This in-the-money value is known as the option's *intrinsic* value. Note that the price (premium) of the option is immaterial.

- An XYZ 50 call is *out* of the money when XYZ is trading at less than 50. If XYZ is 46.25, then the 50 call is 3.75 points out of the money. The option has no intrinsic value. Again, the price of the option itself makes no difference.

- If XYZ is trading exactly at 50, then the 50 call is *at* the money. Someone exercising the call and immediately selling the stock would have neither a profit nor a loss. An at-the-money call (like an out-of-the-money call) has no intrinsic value.

Puts

A put is

- In the money when the strike price is higher than the underlying's market price.
- Out of the money when the strike price is lower than the underlying's market price.
- At the money when the strike price and the market price are equal.

  Example: An ABC 35 put is
- 2.50 points *in* the money when ABC is trading at 32.50.
- 3.25 points *out* of the money when ABC is trading at 38.25.
- *At* the money when ABC is trading at 35.

Margining Equity Options

Long options cannot be margined; they have no loan value and must be paid for in full. Only short options may be margined.

The margin requirement for short equity options is 20 percent of the value of the underlying stock (reduced by any out of the money amount, but not less than 10 percent of the underlying's value) plus the premium.

Note: You must calculate 20 percent of the market value of 100 shares of the underlying stock, not 20 percent of the value of the strike price.

Example: What is the margin requirement for 10 short 50 calls when the underlying stock is trading at 51.50 and the options are trading at 5.75?

- Twenty percent of the value of 1,000 shares of the underlying stock is $10,300 (.2 × $51,500). Ten calls "cover" 1,000 shares.
- Since the option is in the money, the basic requirement cannot be reduced. Adding the premiums gives a total requirement of $16,050 ($10,300 + $5,750). Ten calls at 5.75 each cost a total of $5,750.
- What is the margin requirement for a short 95 put when the premium is 4.25 and the underlying is trading at 97?
- Twenty percent of the value of 100 shares of the underlying is $1,940 (.2 × $9,700).
- The option is out of the money by 2 points, so the basic requirement of $1,940 may be reduced by $200 to $1,740. Adding the premium of $425 gives a total margin requirement of $2,165 ($1,740 + $425).
- What is the margin requirement for 10 short 60 calls when the underlying is trading at 45.00 and the option is priced at .25?
- Twenty percent of the underlying is $9,000 (.2 × $45,000).
- The option is out of the money by 15.00 points, so the basic requirement for each option can be reduced, but not by as much as $1,500. It cannot be reduced to less than 10 percent of the underlying's value. Ten percent of total market value is $4,500, so we can reduce the basic requirement only to that level. Adding the basic requirement to the premium gives a total margin requirement of $4,750 ($4,500 + $250).

SELF-TEST

A. What is the margin requirement for 5 CYA 15 short calls when CYA is trading at 16.00 and the calls are at 2.50?

B. What is the margin requirement for 10 RFQ 30 short puts when RFQ is trading at 31.50 and the puts are at .40?

ANSWERS TO SELF-TEST

A. $2,850. For a single option, the basic requirement is 20 percent of the underlying stock's current market value, or $320 (0.2 × $1,600). Since the options are in the money, the basic requirement cannot be reduced. Adding the premium gives a total requirement of $570 ($320 + $250) for a single option and $2,850 for 5 options.

B. $5,200. For a single option, the requirement is 20 percent of the underlying stock's current market value, or $630 (0.2 × $3,150). Since the options are 1.50 points out of the money, the basic requirement can be reduced by $150 to $480. Adding the premium of $40.00 gives a total requirement of $520 for a single option and $5,200 for 10 options.

Maintenance Requirements

As we have seen, margin requirements are based on three factors: the option's premium, the price of the underlying, and the amount by which the option may be out of the money. In a volatile market, all three of these factors can change fairly dramatically overnight. Brokerage firms must monitor all these changes so as to ensure that the options are properly margined on an ongoing basis.

Example: Let's use, in our explanation, the RFQ 30 puts in question B of the previous "Self-Test." We determined that the required equity was $5,200 for the 10 puts. The client met the call by depositing $4,800 in cash—the sale of the 10 options at $40 each was credited to the account when the options were written (sold)—and thus the two amounts met the $5,200 margin call, and there is now that amount of cash in the account.

Several days later there are dramatic developments and RFQ goes down 2.50 points and closes at 29.00. The puts are also up (remember, they are a *derivative*) and close at 2.10. The puts are now in the money. The *new* margin requirement is 20 percent of the market value of the underlying minus any out-of-the-money value plus the premium. Adding it all up, the new requirement (for just a single option) is $580 (.2 × $2,900) + $210 (the new premium) for a total per-option requirement of $790. The requirement can no longer be reduced because the put options are now in the money. The requirement is thus $790 for one option and $7,900 for all 10 puts. Since there is only $5,200 in cash in the account (see previous paragraph), the client will now be required to deposit an additional $2,700 to bring the cash balance to the now-required $7,900.

Margining Foreign Currency Options

For short foreign currency options, the required margin is the premium plus 4.0 percent of the value of the underlying. Margin may be reduced for out-of-the-money options, but never below the premium plus 0.75 percent of the underlying.

Margining Index Options

Margin required for short index options is the premium plus

- Twenty percent of the index value for narrow-based indexes.
- Or fifteen percent of the index value for broad-based indexes.

As is the case with all other types of options, the basic requirement can be reduced for out-of-the-money options, but it can be no lower than the premium plus 10 percent of the index value.

Example: What is the required margin for a short S&P 100 Index 360 call when the premium is 2.90 and the index price is 361.08?

- The index price is 361.08, which translates to $36,108.
- Since we are dealing with a broad-based index, we use 15 percent of this value as the basic requirement, $5,416.20 (0.15 × $36,108).
- The premium, in dollars, is $290.
- Adding the premium to 15 percent of the index value gives a total margin requirement of $5,706.20 ($5,416.20 + $290).

Note: Series 7 test-takers, this chapter has dealt with the figuration of the margin requirement for various short option positions. If you are asked for the margin call *rather than for the margin* requirement, *you do not add in the premium. Keep in mind that when you sell an option, your account is credited with the proceeds of that sale. This puts money into the account, which satisfies at least part of the requirement. The customer thus has to send in, in cash, only the amount by which the total margin requirement exceeds the premium. The requirement includes the premium; the call (the amount of cash the customer must deposit) excludes the premium.*

Chapter 25

FINANCIAL RATIOS

This is one of the longer chapters in this book, longer perhaps than is warranted by the emphasis—or lack of emphasis—placed on the subject of financial ratios on most of the qualifying examinations, CFA excluded. The subject is, however, of great importance when you consider that a corporation's *report card* consists of its balance sheet and income statement. If you are truly interested in a child's progress in school, you should know how to read his or her report card. Similarly, you should know how to read a corporation's report card when deciding whether to hold, buy, or sell (or sell short) a stock. This chapter will help.

The series 7 examination does not place much emphasis on financial ratios. Included in this chapter are only the more important ones that might be tested. There will be no self-tests in this chapter.

Use the balance sheet in Figure 25-1 and the income statement in Figure 25-2 for all the formulas and examples presented.

FIGURE 25-1   Marobeth Corporation balance sheet: December 31, 2009.

Current Assets	
Cash	$ 450,000
Marketable Securities	95,000
Accounts Receivable	1,885,000
Inventory	2,115,000
	4,545,000
Fixed Assets	
Property & plant	3,350,000
Equipment	1,195,000
Prepaid expenses	755,000
	5,300,000

FIGURE 25-1 *(continued)*

Intangible Assets	
Goodwill	950,000
Total Assets:	$10,795,000
Current Liabilities	
Cash dividends payable	$ 150,000
Accounts payable	955,000
Accrued expenses	1,035,000
Accrued taxes	265,000
	2,405,000
Long-Term Liabilities	
9% bonds due 2006	1,000,000
Net Worth	
7% Pfd. ($100 par)	500,000
Common stock ($1 par)	1,900,000
Capital surplus	300,000
Retained earnings	4,690,000
	7,390,000
Total Liabilities and Net Worth:	$10,795,000

FIGURE 25-2 Marobeth Corporation income statement: January 1–December 31, 2009.*

Net Sales	$14,488,000
− Cost of goods sold	10,915,000
− Selling, general and administrative expenses	1,095,000
− Depreciation	886,000
Operating Income	1,592,000
+ Other income	27,000
Total Income (EBIT)	1,619,000
− Interest on bonds	90,000
− Taxes	509,000
Net Income	1,020,000
− Preferred dividends	35,000
Net Earnings	$ 985,000

*Marobeth common stock is currently trading at 9.88 and is paying an annual dividend of $0.08 per share.

Working Capital

Working capital, a dollar figure, measures the excess of current assets over current liabilities:

Working capital = current assets − current liabilities

Broadly speaking, current assets include cash and items that will become cash within the coming year. Current liabilities include the amounts that the company expects to pay out within the year. There should be an excess of incoming cash over expected expenses.

Example: See Figure 25-1.

Working capital = current assets − current liabilities
= $4,545,000 − $2,405,000 = $2,140,000

Marobeth's working capital is $2,140,000.

Current Ratio

The current ratio shows the relationship between current assets and current liabilities—how many times the current assets are greater than the current liabilities. It is expressed as a ratio, not in dollars and cents.

Current ratio = current assets ÷ current liabilities

Example: See Figure 25-1.

Current ratio = $4,545,000 ÷ $2,405,000 = 1.9 to 1

Marobeth's current ratio is 1.9 to 1.

CALCULATOR GUIDE

▶ 4545000 ÷ 2405000 = ◀ **1.8898128** (1.9 to 1)

Quick Assets

Expressed as a dollar figure, quick assets indicate the total amount of money that a company could muster on short notice. Typically they include all current assets except inventory. Inventory is excluded because other current asset items are rather easily converted to cash, whereas inventories are considered relatively illiquid.

Quick assets = current assets − inventory

Example: See Figure 25-1.

Quick assets = \$4,545,000 − \$2,115,000 = \$2,430,000

Marobeth's quick assets are \$2,430,000.

Quick-Asset Ratio

Sometimes called the *liquidity ratio* or *acid-test ratio*, the quick-asset ratio measures a company's ability to remain solvent—to quickly pay its near-term obligations.

Quick-asset ratio = quick assets ÷ current liabilities

Example: See Figure 25-1.

Quick-asset ratio = \$2,430,000 ÷ \$2,405,000 = 1.0 to 1

The quick-asset ratio for Marobeth is 1.0 to 1.

CALCULATOR GUIDE

▶ 2430000 ÷ 2405000 = ◀ **1.010395** (1.0 to 1)

Capitalization

A company's capitalization shows its source of funding. It is found by adding together long-term debt, preferred stock, and common stockholders' equity.
Common stockholders' equity usually has three components:

● The common-stock account (number of common shares outstanding × par value)
● The capital surplus account
● Retained earnings (earned surplus)

Since net worth includes the preferred stock account and all three elements of the common stock account, we can arrive at capitalization by adding long-term liabilities and net worth:

Capitalization = long-term liabilities + net worth

Example: See Figure 25-1.

Capitalization = $1,000,000 + $7,390,000 = $8,390,000

Marobeth's capitalization is $8,390,000.

Capitalization Ratios

The capitalization ratios show the percentage of the company's total capitalization represented by

- Common stock (the common-stock ratio)
- Preferred stock (the preferred-stock ratio)
- Bonds (the bond ratio)

The three ratios add to 100 percent.

Common-Stock Ratio

The common stockholders' equity is divided by the company's total capitalization:

> Common-stock ratio = stockholders' equity
> ÷ total capitalization

As noted previously, common stockholders' equity has three components:

- The common-stock account (number of common shares outstanding × par value)
- The capital surplus account
- Retained earnings (earned surplus)

> Common stockholders' equity = common stock
> + capital surplus + retained earnings

Example: See Figure 25-1. What is Marobeth's common stock ratio?

- First calculate common stockholders' equity:

> Common stockholders' equity = $1,900,000
> + $300,000 + $4,690,000 = $6,890,000

Common stockholders' equity is $6,890,000.

- Then apply the formula:

$$\text{Common-stock ratio} = \text{stockholders' equity} \div \text{total capitalization}$$
$$= \$6,890,000 \div \$8,390,000$$
$$= 82 \text{ percent}$$

The common stock ratio is 82 percent.

CALCULATOR GUIDE

▶ 1900000 + 300000 + 4690000 ÷ 8390000 × 100 = ◀
82.12157 (82 percent)

Preferred Stock Ratio

The preferred stock ratio shows the percentage of the corporation's total capitalization represented by preferred stock:

$$\text{Preferred-stock ratio} = \text{preferred stock} \div \text{total capitalization}$$

Example: See Figure 25-1.

$$\text{Preferred-stock ratio} = \$500,000 \div \$8,390,000$$
$$= 6 \text{ percent}$$

The preferred-stock ratio is 6 percent.

CALCULATOR GUIDE

▶ 500000 ÷ 8390000 × 100 = ◀ **5.95947** (6 percent)

Bond Ratio

The bond ratio shows the percentage of total capitalization represented by long-term debt:

$$\text{Bond ratio} = \text{bonds} \div \text{total capitalization}$$

Example: See Figure 25-1.

Bond ratio = \$1,000,000 ÷ \$8,390,000 = 12 percent

Marobeth's bond ratio is 12 percent.

CALCULATOR GUIDE

▶ 1000000 ÷ 8390000 × 100 = ◀ **11.91895** (12 percent)

The three capitalization ratios should add to 100 percent.

Example: In the three preceding examples we arrived at

Common-stock ratio	82 percent
Preferred-stock ratio	6 percent
Bond ratio	12 percent
	100 percent

Inventory-Turnover Ratio

The inventory-turnover ratio shows how many times the inventory is "turned over" (sold) during the year:

Inventory-turnover ratio = net sales ÷ inventory

Note: This computation is simplified; accountants would use a much more sophisticated technique.

Example: Refer to Figures 25-1 and 25-2.

Inventory-turnover ratio = $14,488,000
÷ $2,115,000 = 6.85 times

The inventory-turnover ratio for Marobeth is 6.85 times.

CALCULATOR GUIDE

▶ 14488000 ÷ 2115000 = ◀ **6.8501182** (6.85 times)

Margin of Profit

The margin of profit, or *operating ratio*, shows the percentage of operating income to sales—how much is left after expenses.

Margin of profit = operating income ÷ net sales

Example: Refer to Figure 27-2.

Margin of profit = $1,592,000 ÷ $14,488,000
= 11 percent

Marobeth's margin of profit is 11 percent.

CALCULATOR GUIDE

▶ 1592000 ÷ 14488000 × 100 = ◀ **10.9884** (11 percent)

Expense Ratio

This is the flip side of the operating ratio. The expense ratio shows the percentage of sales that were expended before arriving at operating income:

Expense ratio = cost of good sold + selling, general and administrative expenses + depreciation ÷ net sales

Example: See Figure 25-2.

Expense ratio = $10,915,000 + $1,095,000 + $886,000 ÷ $14,488,000 = 89 percent

CALCULATOR GUIDE

▶ 10915000 + 1095000 + 886000 ÷ 14488000 × 100 = ◀ **89.01159** (89 percent)

The two ratios, margin of profit and expense ratio, should add to 100 percent. We can check our last two calculations by adding them together:

Margin of profit	11 percent
Expense ratio	89 percent
	100 percent

Cash Flow

Since depreciation is a noncash expense, cash flow gives a truer picture of the company's actual cash position before dividends are paid:

Cash flow = net income + depreciation

Example: See Figure 25-2.

Cash flow = $1,020,000 + $886,000 = $1,906,000

Cash flow for Marobeth is $1,906,000.

Earnings per Share

Expressed as a dollar figure, earnings per share shows the company's results per share of common stock outstanding.

It is sometimes called *earnings available for common stock-holders* because it is calculated after all other expenses, including interest on bonds, taxes, and preferred dividend payments. It is calculated by dividing net earnings by the number of common shares outstanding:

Earnings per share = net earnings ÷ number of
common shares outstanding

To arrive at the number of common shares outstanding, refer to the balance sheet, specifically the "Net Worth" section. This shows the overall value of the company's common stock and its par value. To find out the number of common shares outstanding, divide the common stock account by the par value of the common shares:

Common stock shares outstanding
= common stock account ÷ par value

Example: See Figures 25-1 and 25-2. First, find the number of shares of common stock outstanding. The common-stock account in Figure 25-1 shows $1,900,000 and indicates a par value of $1 per share.

Common-stock shares outstanding = $1,900,000
÷ $1 = 1,900,000 shares

Now you can calculate earnings per share. Figure 25-2 shows total net earnings of $985,000.

Earnings per share = net earnings ÷ number of
common shares outstanding
= $985,000 ÷ $1,900,000 = $0.52
per share

Marobeth's earnings per share are $0.52.

Earnings Comparisons

To compare per-share earnings results on a year-to-year basis, do the following:

- Subtract the previous year's per-share earnings from the current year's per-share earnings.
- Divide by the previous year's figure.

Earnings comparison = (current earnings −
prior earnings) ÷ prior earnings

Example: Last year's per-share earnings were $0.40, and the current year's per-share earnings are $0.52 (see the preceding example).

$$(\$0.52 - \$0.40) \div \$0.40 = + 30 \text{ percent}$$

The company's per-share earnings were up 30 percent over the previous year's results.

CALCULATOR GUIDE

▶ .52 − .40 ÷ .40 × 100 = ◀ **30.** (30 percent)

Price-Earnings (PE) Ratio

The P/E ratio—a most important measurement—shows the multiple of the per-share market price of the common stock compared with the stock's earnings per share. It shows by how many times the market price exceeds the earnings per share. It is used as a gauge of the relative "expensiveness" of a stock.

P/E ratio = market price per share ÷ earnings per share

Example: See Figure 25-2. The footnote to the income statement shows the current market price for the common stock to be 9.88.

$$\text{P/E ratio} = \$9.88 \div \$.52 = 19 \text{ times}$$

Marobeth's P/E ratio is 19 times. The market price is 19 times greater than the earnings per share.

CALCULATOR GUIDE

▶ 9.88 ÷ .52 = ◀ **19.** (19 times)

Payout Ratio

The percentage of the earnings per share that the corporation pays out in common-stock dividends is expressed by the payout ratio:

Payout ratio = dividend per common share
÷ earnings per common share

Example: See Figure 25-2. The footnote to the income statement shows the common stock's dividend per share to be $0.08. The earnings per share were calculated at $0.52 in a preceding example.

Payout ratio = $0.08 ÷ $0.52 = 15 percent

Marobeth pays out 15 percent of its earnings per share in dividends.

CALCULATOR GUIDE

▶ 0.08 ÷ 0.52 × 100 = ◀ **15.38461** (15 percent)

Chapter 26

TAX-LOSS CARRYFORWARDS

Note: Every year sees changes in the tax code. Investors are encouraged to stay as current as possible with these changes and to always seek competent professional tax counsel.

Capital Gains and Losses

No matter how actively an investor trades, only two capital gains figures need be maintained, a net short-term amount and a net long-term amount. All short-term trades are netted out on a continuing basis; all long-term trades are also netted out.

Example: An investor sells a stock, creating a short-term gain of $500. She later sells another security, producing a short-term loss of $360. It is not necessary to keep a record of both the short-term gain and the short-term loss; all she needs to do is net them out to a single short-term figure of a $140 gain ($500 gain − $360 loss = $140 gain). If the investor then has a $450 short-term loss, she nets the previous balance of +$140 with the new loss of $450 to arrive at a new net figure of an overall short-term loss of $310 (+$140 − $450 = −$310).

Long-term gains and losses are treated in a similar manner. Net all long-term transactions as they occur so that you are carrying only a single net long-term figure, either a profit or a loss.

Example: An investor executes a number of trades in a given year, resulting in the following capital gains and losses. At year end, what is the investor's net tax position?

1. January $500 short-term loss
2. March $1,250 long-term gain
3. April $2,350 short-term gain
4. May $800 short-term loss
5. July $3,150 short-term loss
6. September $900 long-term loss
7. October $4,350 long-term gain

At year end, the investor has a net $2,100 short-term loss and a net $4,700 long-term profit. Here's what the investor's tax records should have shown just after each of the trades listed:

Short Term	Long Term
1. $500 loss	no long-term gain or loss
2. $500 loss	$1,250 gain
3. $1,850 gain	$1,250 gain
4. $1,050 gain	$1,250 gain
5. $2,100 loss	$1,250 term gain
6. $2,100 loss	$350 gain
7. $2,100 loss	$4,700 gain

At year end, the investor has both a short-term loss of $2,100 and a long-term gain of $4,700.

When an investor ends the tax year with both a profit and a loss, the two figures are again netted out to reduce the final capital gains tax picture to a single number. This final number:

- Can be positive (a gain) or negative (a loss).
- Is short term if the short-term gains or losses exceed the long-term gains or losses.
- Is long term if the long-term gains or losses exceed the short-term gains or losses. In other words, the final figure takes on the character of the larger of the two gains or losses.

Example: In the preceding example, the investor would report a net long-term gain of $2,600 for the entire tax year. This figure was arrived at by netting out the $2,100 short-term loss and the $4,700 long-term gain ($-2,100 + $4,700 = +$2,600). It is a *long-term* gain because the long-term gains exceeded the short-term losses.

If an investor has both short- and long-term profits or both short- and long-term losses, they are kept separate.

The only situation in which short- and long-term transactions are netted together is when one is positive (a gain) and the other negative (a loss).

SELF-TEST

Show the investor's final reported capital gains figure(s) for each of the following situations.

A. Short-term gain: $4,500
Long-term loss: $1,250
B. Short-term loss: $1,200
Long-term gain: $3,000
C. Short-term gain: $2,800
Long-term loss: $3,500
D. Short-term loss: $900
Long-term gain: $300
E. Short-term gain: $3,250
Long-term gain: $1,500
F. Short-term loss: $850
Long-term loss: $1,500

ANSWERS TO SELF-TEST

A. Short-term gain of $3,250
B. Long-term gain of $1,800
C. Long-term loss of $700
D. Short-term loss of $600
E. Short-term gain of $3,250 and long-term gain of $1,500
F. Short-term loss of $850 and long-term loss of $1,500

Deduction of Capital Losses

Capital losses are deductible, within certain annual limits. Both short- and long-term losses may be deducted, but short-term losses must be deducted before long-term losses. The annual maximum for *net* deductible losses is $3,000—whether short term, long term, or some of each.

Whatever amount of losses exceeds the annual limit may be carried forward to be deducted in later years.

Example: An investor loses a total of $5,000 short term in 2008. He is allowed to deduct $3,000 against ordinary income in 2008 and carry forward the balance of the loss, $2,000, to 2009. He begins 2009 with a short-term loss of $2,000. If he has no other capital gains and losses in 2009, he deducts the remaining $2,000 against his ordinary income in that year.

Losses retain their short- or long-term character when carried forward. Short-term-loss carryforwards do not "age" to become long term. Remember that short-term losses are to be used first.

Example: Joseph Meehan ends the tax year with $490 in short-term losses. He deducts $490 from his ordinary income in that tax year.

Had Mr. Meehan ended the tax year with $3,600 in short-term losses, he would have deducted the maximum of $3,000 in the current year and carried forward the remaining $600 of short-term loss to the following year.

Carol Treanor ended 2008 with long-term losses of $3,800. She may deduct $3,000 in 2008 and carry forward $800 as a long-term loss to 2009.

If, instead, Ms. Treanor had total long-term losses of $7,500 in 2008, she may deduct $3,000 in that year and carry forward $4,500 to be used in subsequent years. If she had no other capital transactions during the next several years, she would deduct an additional $3,000 in 2009 and the remaining $1,500 in 2010. Thus she would have deducted the entire loss of $7,500 spread over 3 tax years.

Frank Beretta ended 2007 with $900 in short-term losses and $3,500 in long-term losses. He may deduct all $900 of the short-term loss but only $2,100 of the long-term loss in 2007, thus using up his maximum deduction of $3,000. This leaves Mr. Beretta with a long-term tax loss carryforward of $1,400 ($3,500 − $2,100) for 2008.

If, instead, Mr. Beretta had ended 2007 with $3,200 in short-term losses and $1,500 in long-term losses, he would have deducted $3,000 of the short-term loss in 2007 and carried forward the remaining $200 of short-term loss and the entire $1,500 of long-term loss to subsequent years.

SELF-TEST

For each of the following year-end situations, show the deduction for the current tax year and the carryforward(s), if any, for subsequent years. Indicate whether the carry-forwards are short- or long-term losses.

A. Short-term gain of $2,000 and long-term loss of $3,850

B. Short-term loss of $3,500 and long-term loss of $4,000

C. Short-term gain of $450 and long-term loss of $5,400

D. Short-term loss of $2,500 and long-term loss of $3,500

E. Short-term loss of $800 and long-term loss of $1,500

ANSWERS TO SELF-TEST

A. Deduct $1,850; no carryforwards.

B. Deduct $3,000; carry forward $500 short-term loss and $4,000 long-term loss.

C. Deduct $3,000; carry forward $1,950 long term-loss (the short-term gain and the long-term loss net out to a long-term loss of $4,950).

D. Deduct $3,000; carry forward $3,000 long-term loss.

E. Deduct $2,300; no carryforwards.

A Final Word

The mathematics of the securities industry can be bewildering to the uninitiated but second nature to the practiced. We urge you to review the formulas presented as often as you need to until you are able to apply them to real-world situations.

Those preparing for a successful taking of the stockbroker's (the series 7) examination must be able to answer the majority of the "Self-Test" questions correctly. Private investors are also well advised to master as much of the text as possible. They will be better able to monitor their investments, to read and understand the financial press, and to interact more professionally with their brokers and investment advisors.

Success in your investment endeavors!

CALCULATOR GUIDE

▶ Mrc Mrc on/c on/c ◀ **0.** (the end)

ANSWERS TO PRACTICAL EXERCISES

Chapter 3

1. $103,500.

   103:16 = 103$^{16}/_{32}$ = 103½ = $1,035.
   100 × $1,035. = $103,500.
   [100 bonds (100 M) at $1,035. each]

2. $243,125.

   97:08 = 97$^{8}/_{32}$ = 97¼ = $972.50
   250 × $972.50 = $243,125.
   [250 bonds (250 M) at $972.50 each]

3. $997,500.

   99:24 = 99$^{24}/_{32}$ = 99¾ = $997.50
   1,000 × $997.50 = $997,500.
   [1,000 bonds (1 MM) at $997.50 each]

4. The interest would be taxable by the federal government but not taxable by the state. The same situation obtains for Treasury bills, Treasury bonds, and savings bonds.

5. Capital gains are fully taxable. While *interest* on municipal bonds and Treasury issues may be fully or partially exempt from tax, all *capital gains* earned outside a tax-sheltered account such as an IRA are fully taxable.

6. The notes are not callable. Treasury bills and Treasury notes are never callable; some Treasury *bonds* are callable.

Chapter 4

1. Wednesday, July 15. The settlement date (when payment is due) will be the third business day after the trade date. If there are no intervening holidays, stocks trades effected on Monday settle that Thursday; Tuesday's trades settle that Friday; Wednesday's trades settle the following Monday; Thursday's trades settle the following Tuesday; Friday's trades settle the following Wednesday.

2. Yes, the investor will receive the dividend. With a record date of Wednesday, July 15, the ex-dividend date will be set 2 business days earlier, Monday, July 13. Stock purchased *before* the ex dividend (in this case, July 10) is entitled to the dividend.

3. There is no particular holding period. There is no such restriction. So long as a client is not "kiting" (buying stock with no intention of paying for it), stock may be sold immediately after being purchased.

4. The amount of the dividend was set by the company's board of directors.

5. The ex-dividend date was set by the New York Stock Exchange. Ex-dividend dates are set by whichever floor-based exchange trades the stock. The NASD sets the ex-dividend dates for Nasdaq-traded and OTC stocks.

6. The record date was set by the company's board of directors.

Chapter 5

1. $239,437.50. The bonds are worth, respectively:

ABC	$10,712.50 (10 × $1,071.25)
DEF	$10,350.00 (10 × $1,035.00)
GHI	$97,750.00 (100 × $977.50)
JKL	$120,625.00 (100 × $1,206.25)

The total comes to $239,437.50.

2. $19,600. Each year the bonds will pay, respectively:

ABC	$600 (6 percent × $10,000)
DEF	$500 (5 percent × $10,000)
GHI	$8,500 (8.5 percent × $100,000)
JKL	$10,000 (10 percent × $100,000)

The total comes to $19,600.

3. The bond portfolio's market value would *decline* sharply. When interest rates rise, the market prices of fixed-income securities decline; when interest rates decline, the market prices of fixed-income securities rise.

Chapter 6

1. $97.22. The bonds pay interest each April and October 1. The last-paid coupon prior to the trade was October 1; therefore, the seller is owed interest from that date through the day before settlement.

   A corporate bond trade on Tuesday, November 18, settles on Friday, November 21 (T + 3). The seller is due interest for the full month of October (at 30 days per month) and the first 20 days of November (up to, but not including, the settlement date), that is, 30 + 20 = 50 days of accrued interest. The annual interest on 10 M 7 percent bonds is $700. ($10,000 × 7 percent). When calculating accrued interest on corporate and municipal bonds, we use a 360-day year. The accrued interest formula is ($700. × 50) ÷ 360 = $97.22.

2. $11,722.22. "Final money" consists of both the principal amount (1,162.50 × 10 = $11,625.) and the accrued interest ($97.22).

3. $11,625. His tax-cost basis does *not* include the accrued interest, just the principal amount.

4. $15,625.00. The bonds pay interest February 15 and August 15. The last-paid coupon prior to the trade was August 15; therefore, the seller is owed interest from that date through the day before settlement.

   A government bond trade on Monday, December 7, settles on Tuesday, December 8 (T + 1). The seller is due interest for part of August; the full months of September, October, and November; and the first 7 days in December. From August 15 through August 31 *inclusive*, there are 17 days; we use the actual days in September (30), October (31), and November (31) and 7 days in December (up to, but not including, the settlement date), that is, 17 + 30 + 31 + 31 + 7 = 115 days of accrued interest.

   Important point: Since we begin counting on August 15, there are *17 days* of accrued interest in August, counting from the fifteenth through the thirty-first, *inclusively*.

The next step is to determine the actual number of days in the half year in which the bond was traded (August 15 to February 15): August, 17 days (see above); September, 30 days; October, 31 days; November, 30 days; December, 31 days; January, 31 days; and February, 14 days (we do not count February 15, which begins a new interest period). Thus $17 + 30 + 31 + 30 + 31 + 31 + 14 = 184$ days in the half year in which the bond was traded. The annual interest on 1 MM of 5 percent bonds is $50,000. ($1,000,000 \times 5$ percent). Since we are using the number of days in the *half* year during which the bond was traded, we also use only *half* a year's interest when figuring the accrued interest on a government bond trade. A half year's interest on this bond would be $25,000.

Applying the accrued-interest formula for government bonds: a half year's interest multiplied by the number of days of accrued interest, divided by the number of days in the half year of the trade, we get

$$\$25,000. \times 115 \div 184 = \$15,625.00$$

Chapter 9

1. 11.31 percent. Read *down* the 11-year column and *across* the 96.50 row. The answer is found where the column and row intersect.
2. $1,005. Read *down* the 10-year column to the figure 10.671, and then read across to the left to the price column, which reads 100.50. This price, in dollars, equals $1,005.
3. 9.30 percent. Here, 9½ years would be the average of the 9-year yield (9.25 percent) and the 10-year yield (9.35 percent).
4. $972.50. A price of 97.00 gives a yield of 11.21 percent. A price of 97.50 gives a yield of 11.13 percent. An 11.17 percent basis is halfway between the two—97.25. A price of 97.25 translates to a dollar value of $972.50 per $1,000 par-value bond.

Chapter 10

1. 8.29 percent. An 8 percent bond pays $80 annually; a bond priced at 96½ sells for $965. Thus

$$\frac{\$80}{\$965} = 8.29 \text{ percent}$$

2. 8.50 percent. To the numerator we *add* the annualized discount of $3.50 [($1,000 − $965) ÷ 10]. The denominator is the average of the purchase price and par, $982.50 ($965 + $1,000) ÷ 2 = $982.50. Thus

$$\frac{\$80 + \$3.50}{\$982.50} = \frac{\$83.50}{\$982.50} = 8.50 \text{ percent}$$

3. The yield to call will be *greater* than the yield to maturity. The yield to call is always greater than the yield to maturity for bonds trading at a discount.

4. 5.85 percent. A 6 percent bond pays $60 annually; a bond priced at 102.50 sells for $1,025. Thus

$$\frac{\$60}{\$1,025} = 5.85 \text{ percent}$$

5. 5.43 percent. From the numerator we *subtract* the annualized premium of $5 [($1,025 − $1,000) ÷ 5]. The denominator is the average of the purchase price and par, $1,012.50 [($1,025 + $1,000) ÷ 2]. Thus

$$\frac{\$60 - \$5}{\$1,012.50} = \frac{\$55}{\$,1012.50} = 5.43 \text{ percent}$$

6. The yield to call will be *less* than the yield to maturity. The yield to call at par is always less than the yield to maturity for bonds trading at a premium.

Chapter 12

1. The municipal bond will give the greater after-tax yield. Dividing the tax-exempt yield by (100 percent minus the investor's tax bracket) gives the *taxable equivalent yield*:

$$4.35 \div (100 \text{ percent} - 30 \text{ percent})$$
$$= 4.35 \div .70 = 6.21 \text{ percent}$$

This indicates that, for an investor in the 30 percent tax bracket, a corporate bond would have to offer a

yield of 6.21 percent to equal the tax free yield of
4.35 percent afforded by the municipal bond.

There is no particular tax exemption on interest paid
on corporate bonds if they are incorporated in the
investor's home state.

2. The corporate bond. Interest payments received in
IRA accounts are not taxed at the time of receipt,
whether paid on taxable or tax-free bonds, so there
is no particular tax advantage for munis in an IRA or
other tax-sheltered retirement account.

Chapter 14

1. $15.83. The legal maximum charge for a
noncontractual plan is 8.50 percent of the offering
price.

$$\text{Offer price} = \frac{\text{net asset value}}{100 \text{ percent} - \text{sales charge percent}}$$

$$\text{Offer price} = \frac{\$14.48}{100 \text{ percent} - 8.50 \text{ percent}}$$

$$\text{Offer price} = \frac{\$14.48}{.915} = \$15.83$$

2. 6.0 percent.

$$\$13.28 - \$12.48 = \$0.80 \text{ (the sales charge)}$$

$$\frac{\$0.80}{\$13.28} = 6.0 \text{ percent}$$

3. 2,944.063 shares. The 3 percent sales charge applies
to the *entire* purchase. Thus

$$\frac{\$9.88}{100 \text{ percent} - 3 \text{ percent}} = \frac{\$9.88}{.97} = \$10.19 \text{ offer price}$$

$$\frac{\$30,000}{\$10.19} = 2,944.063 \text{ shares}$$

Chapter 15

1. She will receive 150 subscription rights. That's the rule; an investor always receives one right per old share held.

2. She is entitled to subscribe for 30 new shares. Since there are 5,000,000 "old" shares outstanding and the company is going to issue 1,000,000 new shares ($1/5$ as many as are currently outstanding), investors are entitled to subscribe for $1/5$ the number of shares they currently own. The client owns 150 shares and may subscribe for $1/5$ that number of new shares ($1/5 \times 150$), or 30 additional shares.

3. $2,370. Thirty new shares (see preceding answer) at $79.00 per share will cost a total of $2,370.

4. She should sell the rights. Investors who choose not to *use* their rights are best advised to sell them. The rights have a value and should not be ignored. Either subscribe to the additional shares or sell the rights.

Chapter 16

1. His total quarterly dividend will be $100. An 8 percent preferred stock ($50 par) pays $4.00 per share annually (8 percent $\times$ $50). Thus the total *annual* dividend on the 100 shares will be $400, and each *quarterly* dividend will be for $1/4$ that amount, or $100.

2. A total of 250 shares of Mahan Company common stock if all 100 shares of preferred stock were exchanged. A $50 par preferred stock with a conversion *price* of 20.00 has a conversion *ratio* of 2.5 ($50 \div 20.00 = 2.5$). For each share of preferred stock converted, the holder would receive 2.5 shares of common stock.

3. The yield on this convertible preferred stock will be lower. This is the "cost" to the purchaser of a convertible preferred stock; the investor must accept a lower yield than that to be expected from a straight (*nonconvertible*) preferred stock of similar quality.

4. The preferred stock is less secure than the company's bonds but more secure than the

company's common stock. Within a given company,
that's the order: bonds first, then preferred stock,
and common stock last.

Chapter 21

1. $60,000 market value—$30,000 debit balance =
   $30,000 equity. The investor must deposit 50
   percent of the purchase price, which would leave a
   debit balance of $30,000—the amount loaned by the
   brokerage firm.
2. $72,000 market value − $30,000 debit balance =
   $42,000 equity. Note that the market value and the
   equity of the account have both increased by the
   same amount, whereas the debit balance has
   remained unchanged.
3. $6,000. The required equity for an account with
   $72,000 market value is half that amount, or
   $36,000. Note the account now has an equity of
   $42,000 (see preceding answer), which is $6,000
   higher than the requirement. This "excess equity"
   now becomes the SMA.
4. $12,000. With regulation T at its current level of 50
   percent, an account's buying power is double its
   SMA.
5. $40,000. The lowest permissible market value before
   a maintenance call is issued is calculated by
   multiplying the account's debit balance by $4/3$. Thus

$$4/3 \times \$30,000 = \$40,000.$$

Chapter 23

1. The option is in the money. The option enables one
   to exercise (buy) at 65 while the stock is trading at
   66.25. This indicates that the option has a positive
   value and is thus *in* the money.
2. The option has 1.25 points of intrinsic value. An
   option's intrinsic value is equal to its in-the-money
   amount (see preceding answer). Had the stock been
   trading at 65.00, the option would be *at* the money;
   if the stock were trading below 65.00, the option
   would be *out of* the money. In these last two
   instances, the option would have no intrinsic value.

3. The option's time value is 6.25 points. An option's
    time value is the amount by which the option's
    open-market price (premium) exceeds its intrinsic
    value, if any. Since the intrinsic value is 1.25 (see
    preceding explanation), the option's time value is
    6.25 points (premium − intrinsic value: 7.50 − 1.25
    = 6.25) For at-the-money or out-of-the-money
    options (which have no intrinsic value), their
    premiums consist only of time value.

4. Unlimited. At least in theory, there is no limit as to
    how high the underlying stock might rise.

5. $750. The purchaser of an option can only lose the
    amount paid for the option (the premium). An
    option's purchaser has the right to do something but
    is under no obligation to do anything.

6. $750. This is as good as it can get for the option
    writer. He or she can get to keep the premium he or
    she received when he or she wrote the option. Note
    that the option buyer's maximum *loss* potential (see
    preceding explanation) is the same as the option
    writer's *profit* potential.

7. Unlimited. Refer to the explanation for question 4.
    Since options are a zero-sum game, the option
    buyer's maximum profit potential is the same as the
    option writer's maximum loss potential. A naked
    (uncovered) writer is exposed to potentially large
    losses.

8. $7,500. One option trading at 7.50 costs $750. Ten
    such options would cost a total of $7,500.

INDEX OF FORMULAS

This index summarizes the calculations in this book, in many cases giving examples.

Chapter 1
Pricing Stocks

Number of shares × price per share

100 shares trading at 36.75
100 × 36.75 = $3,675 (market value of 100 shares)

Chapter 2
Pricing Corporate Bonds

Par value of bonds × price (as a percentage of par)

$10,000 par value (10 M) at 95³/₄
=10,000 × .9575 = $9,575 (dollar price for 10 bonds)

Chapter 3
Pricing Government Bonds and Notes

Par value of bonds or notes × price
(as a percentage of par)

$1,000,000 par value (1 MM) at 101:08 (101¹/₄)
1,000,000 × 1.0125 = $1,012,500
(dollar price for 1 MM bonds)

Chapter 4
Dividend Payments

Quarterly rate per share × 4

$0.35 quarterly dividend
$0.35 × 4 = $1.40 (annual dividend rate)

Chapter 5
Interest Payments

Par value × coupon rate

$10,000 par value (10 M) bonds with 9 percent coupon
$10,000 × .09 = $900 (annual interest on 10 bonds)

Chapter 6
Accrued Interest: Corporate and Municipal Bonds

$$\text{Annual interest} \times \frac{\text{Number of days from last payment to day before settlement}}{360}$$

$10,000 par value (10 M) 9 percent corporate bond
Interest payment dates: January and July 1
Sold May 2 for settlement May 5

$$\$900 \times \frac{124}{360} = \$310 \text{ (accrued interest on 10 bonds)}$$

All months have 30 days; all years are 360 days.

Accrued Interest: Government Bonds and Notes

$$\text{Semiannual interest} \times \frac{\text{Number of days from last payment to day before settlement}}{\text{Number of days in the half year of the trade}}$$

$1,000,000 par value (1 MM) 8 percent
government bond
Interest payment dates: May and November 15
Sold June 3 for settlement June 4

$$\$40,000 \times \frac{20}{184} = \$4,347.80 \quad \text{(accrued interest on 1 MM bonds)}$$

Use actual days in each month.

Chapter 7
Current Yield

Annual dividend (or interest) ÷ current price

Stock paying $1.20 annually and trading at 18.85
$1.20 ÷ 18.85 = 6.4 percent (current yield)

Chapter 8
Nominal Yield

The same as the coupon rate. Thus 8 percent bonds have a nominal yield of 8.00 percent.

Chapter 9
Yield to Maturity: Basis Pricing

The discount rate at which the present value of all future payments would equal the present price of the bond, assuming that coupons are reinvested at the yield to maturity. Found by using a basis book or an especially programmed calculator (see the yield-basis book in Chapter 9 and Chapter 10 for the rule-of-thumb yield to maturity).

The Yield-Basis Book: Interpretation and Interpolation

Basis books may be used (1) to determine a bond's yield to maturity given its current price or (2) to determine the price of a bond given its yield to maturity. To calculate a yield for a price between those listed in the basis book, set up a proportion. See text for details.

Chapter 10
The Rule-of-Thumb Yield to Maturity

$$\frac{\text{Annual interest} + \text{annualized discount}}{(\text{or} - \text{annualized premium})}{(\text{Current market value} + \$1,000) \div 2}$$

Bond with an 8 percent coupon, 10 years to maturity, priced at .98.

$$\frac{\$80 + (20 \div 10)}{(\$980 + \$1,000) \div 2} = \frac{80 + 2}{\$1,980 \div 2} = \frac{82}{\$990}$$

$$= 8.28 \text{ percent (rule-of-thumb yield to maturity)}$$

Chapter 11
Pricing Municipal Bonds

Municipal bonds are priced either like corporate bonds (see Chapter 2) or on a yield-to-maturity basis (see Chapters 9 and 10).

Chapter 12
Comparing Tax-Free and Taxable Yields

Tax-exempt yield $\div$ (1. $-$ tax bracket percent)

An investor in the 33 percent tax bracket holds a tax-free bond with a yield of 8.5 percent and wishes to know the yield he or she must receive from a taxable bond to receive the equivalent after-tax return.

$$8.50 \div (1. - .33) = 8.50 \div 0.67 = 12.69 \text{ percent}$$
(equivalent taxable yield)

Chapter 13
Pricing Treasury Bills: Discount Yields, Coupon Equivalent Yields

Treasury bills are priced on a discounted yield basis. Converting the quotations into dollar prices is a two-step process:

Discount = par value x price (in decimal form)

$$\times \frac{\text{days to maturity}}{360}$$

Then

Dollar price = par value $-$ discount

What is the dollar price for $1,000,000 Treasury bills maturing in 95 days and trading at 5.42?

$$\$1,000,000 \times .0542 \times \frac{95}{360} = \$14,302.78 \text{ (discount)}$$

$$\$1,000,000 - \$14,302.78 = \$985,697.30 \text{ (dollar price)}$$

Then, to convert to a coupon-equivalent yield:

$$\text{Coupon-equivalent yield} = \frac{\text{discount}}{\text{dollar price}} \times \frac{365}{\text{days to maturity}}$$

$$\frac{\$14,302.78}{\$985,697.30} \times \frac{365}{95} = 5.58 \text{ percent (coupon-equivalent}$$
yield)

Chapter 14
Mutual Funds

Total market value = number of fund shares held
$\times$ bid (NAV) price

AgroProducts Fund is quoted 11.54–12.41. An investor owns 507.452 shares.

$$507.452 \text{ shares} \times \$11.54 = \$5,856 \text{ market value}$$
$$\text{of fund shares held}$$

Net asset value per share = total assets − total liabilities ÷ number of fund shares outstanding

ABC mutual fund has 1,586,000 shares outstanding, total assets of $13,365,000, and total liabilities of $2,013,000.

$$\$13,365,000 - \$2,013,000 \div 1,586,000 =$$
$$\$7.16 \text{ net asset vale (NAV)}$$

Offering price = net asset value ÷ (1 − percent sales charge)

The Treanor Fund has a sales charge of 7 percent and a net asset value of $13.65.

$$\frac{\$13.65}{1 - .07} = \$14.68 \text{ offering price}$$

Sales charges (as a percentage of the offer price)
% Sales sharge = (offer price − net asset value) ÷ offer price

The Chirico Fund is quoted 20.24–22.12.

$$(22.12 - 20.24) \div 22.12 = 8.5 \text{ percent (sales charge)}$$

Redemption fees

Redemption value = (number of shares × NAV) × (1. − percent redemption fee)

The Meehan Fund has a net asset value (NAV) per share of $19.39 and levies a redemption fee of 1 percent. A client redeeming 1200 shares would receive:

$$(1,200 \times \$19.39) \times (1. - .01) = \$23,268 \times 0.99 =$$
$$\$23,035.32 \text{ (net proceeds of redemption)}$$

Breakpoint sales
The sales charge is reduced for certain amounts of "bulk" purchases such as $10,000 or $25,000.

The Cartlidge Fund has a maximum sales charge of 8.5 percent, which reduces to 7.5 percent for purchases of $10,000 to $25,000. The fund is quoted 18.85–20.60. If Marianne Hynd purchases $12,500 of the fund, how many shares will she receive?

The offering price of 20.60 applies only to purchases at the maximum sales charge (8.5 percent). Marianne's entire purchase will be made at the 7.5 percent level.

$$\frac{\$18.85}{1 - \% \text{ sales charge}} = \frac{\$18.85}{1 - .075} = \$20.38$$

(offer price for purchases totaling $10,000 to $25,000)

$$\$12,500 \div \$20.38 = 613.346 \text{ shares}$$
(purchased at the reduced sales charge)

Right of accumulation
Once a breakpoint has been reached through previous purchases, all future purchases are made at the reduced breakpoint level.

Chapter 15
Rights Offerings

Old stock trading with rights (cum rights):
Theoretical value of a right = (market price − subscription price) ÷ (number of rights needed to subscribe to 1 new share) + 1

MNO is offering new shares on a four-for-one basis at 34.00 per share. MNO's "old" stock is trading at 30.00, cum rights.

$$(34 - 30) \div (4 + 1) = \$0.80 \text{ (theoretical value of a right)}$$

Old stock trading without rights (ex rights):
Theoretical value of a right = (market price − subscription price) ÷ number of rights needed to subscribe to 1 new share

PQR is offering new shares on a six-for-one basis at 85.00 per share. PQR's "old" stock is trading at 82.00, ex rights.

$$(85 - 82) \div 6 = \$0.50 \text{ (theoretical value of a right)}$$

Chapter 16
Convertible Securities

Conversion price − conversion ratio

Convertible securities are described as being convertible *at* a specific price. This conversion *price* divided into the convertible security's par value gives the number of common shares into which the security is convertible (the conversion *ratio*).

XYZ convertible preferred is convertible at $50 and has a par value of $100 per share. XYZ convertible preferred has a conversion price of $50 and a conversion ratio of 2. Each share of preferred may be exchanged for 2 shares of common stock.

Parity
When a convertible security and its underlying common stock are in equilibrium.

RFQ convertible bonds are exchangeable for 50 shares of RFQ common stock. The bonds are trading at $106^{1/4}$ and the stock at 21.25. The bond is selling for $1,062.50 and is exchangeable for exactly that same dollar value of common stock because 50 shares of the common stock at 21.25 are also worth $1,062.50 (50 × $21.25 = $1,062.50).

The convertible bond and the common stock into which it is convertible are said to be trading *at parity*.

Arbitrage
When a convertible security is trading at a discount to parity with its underlying stock, there is an opportunity to simultaneously buy the convertible security and sell the underlying stock, thereby locking in a profit. These opportunities are very rare and are almost immediately taken advantage of by professional arbitrageurs.

Refer to the preceding section on parity. If the bonds were trading at 103 rather than $106^{1/4}$, it would be possible to buy the bond for $1,030 and simultaneously sell the underlying 50 shares of stock at 21.25 each. The sale of stock would bring in $1,062.50, which gives the arbitrageur a profit (ignoring commissions) of $32.50 per bond.

Forced conversion
When a convertible issue is called, the owner must determine whether the market value of stock to be received on

conversion exceeds the call price. If he or she would receive more by converting just prior to the call rather than accepting the call, it is known as a *forced* conversion.

MNO convertible bonds are exchangeable for 34 shares of MNO common stock. MNO announces that it is calling the bonds at 102. The common stock is trading at 35.50. If the bondholder accepts the call (does not convert), he or she will receive $1,020 in cash. If he or she does convert, he or she will receive 34 shares of common stock worth $1,207 (34 × 35.50). Thus he or she is "forced" to convert in order to realize the larger dollar value.

Chapter 17
Bond Amortization and Accretion

The tax-cost basis of many bonds changes over time. When the cost basis of a bond purchased at a premium is lowered over time, it is known as *amortization*. Raising the cost basis over time for a bond purchased at a discount is known as *accretion*.

A bond with 10 years remaining to maturity is purchased at 104$^1/_2$. What is the bond's cost basis after being held 5 years?

The bond was purchased for $1,045—a premium of $45. This $45 premium is amortized over the life of the bond so that every year the cost basis of the bond is reduced by one-tenth of the premium, or $4.50. After the bond is held 5 years, the cost basis of the bond has been reduced to $1,022.50 [$1,045 − (5 × $4.50) = $1,045 − $22.50 = $1,022.50].

Accretion (raising the cost basis) is figured in a similar fashion.

Chapter 18
Basic Margin Transactions

Equity in a *long* account:
Long market value − debit balance = equity
Equity in a *short* account:
Credit balance − short market value = equity

Margin calls
Margin calls are generated only when a position is established or increased (long purchases or short sales). The current requirement (regulation T) is 50 percent.

Chapter 19
Excess Equity and the Special Memorandum Account (SMA)

When the equity in a margin account exceeds the requirement, the "excess" equity is transferred to the SMA. Such excess equity, within certain limits, can be used to purchase additional securities without putting up additional cash or may be sent to the client in cash. Either use of the SMA will increase the account's debit balance.

Cash available = the amount of cash that may be sent to the owner of a margin account. It is equal to the SMA, provided that the cash payment does not reduce the account's equity below either 25 percent of market value or $2,000.

Chapter 20
Buying Power

Buying power = the dollar value of securities that may be purchased in a margin account without the client having to send in additional money. The buying power is twice the value of the SMA.

Chapter 21
Maintenance Requirements for Long Accounts

For long accounts the most lenient maintenance requirement is 25 percent. Most brokerages impose stricter requirements such as 30 or 35 percent.

Maintenance calls in a long account may be met by

- A deposit of cash in the amount of the call
- A deposit of marginable securities with a market value of 133 percent the amount of the call
- A sellout of securities in the account having a market value four times the amount of the call

Maintenance excess is the amount by which a margin account's equity exceeds the account's maintenance requirement.

Chapter 22
Maintenance Requirements for Short Accounts

The short account maintenance requirement varies with the price of the short position:

Price of Short Stock	Maintenance Requirement
0 to 2.50	$2.50 per share
2.50 to 5.00	100 percent
5.00 to 16.66	$5.00 per share
16.67 or higher	30 percent

Chapter 23
Pricing Options

Equity options: Priced in dollars and cents, like stocks.

Foreign-currency options: Premiums, strike prices, and underlying currency values are expressed in cents or hundredths of cents.

Index options: Traded in dollars and cents. The most common multiplier is 100.

Chapter 24
Options Margin

Stock options: 20 percent of the market value of the underlying + premium

Foreign-currency options: 4 percent of the market value of the underlying + premium

Index options
   Broad-based: 15 percent of index value + premium
   Narrow-based: 20 percent of index value + premium

Note: The requirement for each of the preceding may be reduced by the amount by which the margined option is out of the money, except that the lower limit to which this may be reduced is

Equity options	10 percent minimum
Foreign-currency options	0.75 percent minimum
Index options	10 percent minimum

Chapter 25
Financial Ratios

Working capital = current assets − current liabilities
Current ratio = current assets ÷ current liabilities
Quick-asset ratio = quick assets ÷ current liabilities
Capitalization = bonds + net worth
Common-stock ratio = common stock + surplus + retained earnings ÷ capitalization

Preferred-stock ratio = preferred stock ÷ capitalization

Bond ratio = bonds ÷ capitalization

Inventory-turnover ratio = sales ÷ inventory

Margin of profit = operating income ÷ sales

Expense ratio = cost of goods + selling, general and admin. expenses + depreciation ÷ sales

Cash flow = net income + depreciation

Earnings per share = net earnings ÷ number of common shares outstanding

Price-earnings ratio = market price per share ÷ earnings per share

Payout ratio = dividend per share ÷ earnings per share

Chapter 26
Tax-Loss Carryforwards

Investors may only deduct, from ordinary income, a maximum of $3,000 of net losses in a single tax year. Any net losses greater than the $3,000 annual limit may be carried forward to subsequent tax years. Short-term losses are used first, then long-term losses.

INDEX